R. Meher

W9-BUY-206

THE DAWN OF
PEACE IN EUROPE

ALSO BY MICHAEL MANDELBAUM

*The Nuclear Question: The United States
and Nuclear Weapons, 1946–1976*

*The Nuclear Revolution: International Politics
Before and After Hiroshima*

The Nuclear Future

Reagan and Gorbachev (With Strobe Talbott)

The Global Rivals (With Seweryn Bialer)

*The Fate of Nations: The Search for National Security in the
Nineteenth and Twentieth Centuries*

MICHAEL MANDELBAUM

THE DAWN
OF PEACE
IN EUROPE

WITH A FOREWORD BY RICHARD C. LEONE

A TWENTIETH CENTURY FUND BOOK

1996 ◆ The Twentieth Century Fund Press ◆ New York

The Twentieth Century Fund sponsors and supervises timely analyses of economic policy, foreign affairs, and domestic political issues. Not-for-profit and nonpartisan, the Fund was founded in 1919 and endowed by Edward A. Filene.

BOARD OF TRUSTEES OF THE TWENTIETH CENTURY FUND

Morris B. Abram
H. Brandt Ayers
Peter A. A. Berle
Alan Brinkley
José A. Cabranes
Joseph A. Califano, Jr.
Alexander Morgan Capron
Hodding Carter III
Edward E. David, Jr.
Brewster C. Denny
Charles V. Hamilton
August Heckscher
Matina S. Horner

Lewis B. Kaden
James A. Leach
Richard C. Leone
P. Michael Pitfield
Richard Ravitch
Arthur M. Schlesinger, Jr.
Harvey I. Sloane, M.D.
Theodore C. Sorensen
James Tobin
David B. Truman
Shirley Williams
William Julius Wilson

Richard C. Leone, *President*

Library of Congress Cataloging-in-Publication Data

Mandelbaum, Michael.
    The dawn of peace in Europe / Michael Mandelbaum.
        p.   cm.
    "A Twentieth Century Fund book."
    Includes bibliographical references (p.) and index.
    ISBN 0–87078–396–3
        1. National security--Europe.   2. North Atlantic Treaty Organization.
    3. Russia (Federation)--Foreign relations--Europe.   4. Europe--Foreign
    relations--Russia (Federation)   5. United States--Foreign relations---
    Europe.   6. Europe--Foreign relations--United States.   I. Title.
    UA646.M37   1996
    355′ .03304--dc20   96-21875

                                                                                    CIP

Cover Design, Illustration, and Graphics: Claude Goodwin
Manufactured in the United States of America.

Copyright © 1996 by Michael Mandelbaum. All rights reserved. No part of this publication may be reproduced, stored in a retrieval system, or transmitted, in any form or by any means, electronic, mechanical, photo-copying, recording, or otherwise, without the prior written permission of the Twentieth Century Fund, Inc.

CONTENTS

*T*o Marcia S. and Robert A. Riesman, in honor of the fiftieth anniversary of their wedding and in appreciation of their many contributions to their community and their country, this book is affectionately dedicated.

FOREWORD

Of course it was all too easy: the sudden and complete collapse of the Soviet empire, the embrace of all things Western, the overnight transformation of Eastern European states into frisky, even coltish, capitalist-democracies. Given the drama and significance of the events since 1986, small wonder that a legion of public intellectuals has been eager to seize the moment, offering explanations, snappy labels, and the obligatory new paradigms. The "end of history" was pronounced for the whole planet; the "dawn of a new era" of international peace and prosperity in Europe was hailed; and in the formerly Communist countries, the miracle cure provided by "shock therapy" was breathlessly anticipated.

A few years later, the same experts, all too often with equal assurance, describe the situation as up for grabs. Perhaps only one question has been answered: primitive tribal hostilities were repressed, not diminished, by decades of Communist control. But the answers to many other questions remain far from clear. Will the Communists return to power in many of these states, as they already have in a few? Will the West discover that it confronts new dangers, albeit probably not direct nuclear threats? Are there other kinds of capitalism that may work, if not ideally, at least well enough to satisfy the very unhappy masses in most of these different lands?

The key to unraveling these unknowns lies, most of all, in the prospects of the nation at the heart of the new region, a shrunken but still critically important Russia. No longer either an enigma or a direct threat, Russia remains, in terms of both its short- and long-term fate, a fascinating and some-times terrifying puzzle to the West. Declines in personal income, personal safety, and life expectancy have created political volatility and ripe opportunities for extremists of every sort. Moreover, for the foreseeable future, Russia could at any time become again the decisive factor in deter-mining American engagement in European and even glob-al security matters.

These uncertainties ensure continued, intense interest in the future of America's central anti-Communist alliance, the North Atlantic Treaty Organization (NATO). NATO's continuing importance is magnified by the simple fact that, in a time when foreign policy initiatives are politically very difficult, it is an institution with a traditionally strong, bipar-tisan base of support. Amidst the present uncertainty about the future architecture of security arrangements in Europe, NATO is, in many ways, the abiding symbol of Western unity and determination. That reputation has survived, mostly intact, the sorry recent history of Bosnia—a tragedy that revealed both the contemporary strengths and weak-nesses of the NATO countries when confronted by a new sort of crisis. There are no Soviet tank forces in Bosnia; for several years, the deadly conflict has been played out in the power vacuum created by the very absence of the threat of those tanks.

The sharpest debate about NATO involves the propos-al to include several of the former satellites of the Soviet Union in the organization. The Clinton administration has taken the lead on this proposal, backed, with varying degrees of enthusiasm, by its alliance partners. It is a proposal that upsets virtually all factions in Russia. The outcome of American, NATO, and UN intervention in Bosnia will determine the short-run political prospects for expansion. But, regardless of events, the issue is likely to stay alive. For some, the proposal arouses the ghosts of the great-power rivalries of the past and sets the stage for sharp disagreements in the future. For others, it is a central part of the reorganization of security arrangements on both sides of the Atlantic.

In this context, the Fund was delighted when Michael Mandelbaum, the Christian A. Herter Professor of American Foreign Policy at The Paul H. Nitze School of Advanced International Studies of The Johns Hopkins University, and one of the key public participants in the debate about European security in general and NATO expansion specifically, offered to prepare a short volume with a sharp focus on the current debate. Mandelbaum, already under contract to produce a Fund book about the new foundations of American security policy, has been a strong and effective critic of the plan to include several formerly Communist nations in NATO in the very near future. In the pages that follow, he presents a tightly reasoned and firmly argued brief for his position. Still, while Mandelbaum has a point of view and argues it forcefully, he does not ignore the case on the other side. His approach is comprehensive, as well as broadly accessible to all those with a keen interest in U.S. policy. Moreover, he offers a fresh way of seeing the post-Cold War world, indicating how, incrementally, we have begun to put in place a new regime of security. These new arrangements, taken together, are working well so far, and they have the potential to grow into a strong security fabric.

This book is in keeping with the Fund's interest in the post-Cold War situation, as evidenced by our support for such examinations as Richard Ullman's *Securing Europe*,

James Chace's *The Consequences of the Peace*, and Jonathan Dean's *Ending Europe's Wars*, as well as a group of forthcoming books: John Ruggie's *Winning the Peace*, Steven Burg's *War or Peace*, and David Calleo's reassessment of Europe's future.

Michael Mandelbaum ranks in the top tier of scholars examining great-power relations. With this book, he makes another significant contribution to the policy debate about the role of the United States in Europe. On behalf of the Trustees of the Twentieth Century Fund, I thank him for his especially timely effort.

RICHARD C. LEONE, *PRESIDENT*
The Twentieth Century Fund
May 1996

ACKNOWLEDGMENTS

The Dawn of Peace in Europe originated as part of a book on the future of American foreign policy sponsored by the Twentieth Century Fund. I am grateful to the Fund's president, Richard C. Leone, for supporting the idea of turning what began as a chapter into a book-length study.

In addition to the Twentieth Century Fund, I am indebted to three other institutions. The Carnegie Corporation of New York, and its president, David Hamburg, and the Aspen Institute, and its senior fellow and creator and director of its Congressional Program, Dick Clark, have given me the opportunity to discuss the problems of European security with scholars and policymakers from both Europe and the United States over the past decade. At the Council on Foreign Relations I have directed, also with the assistance of the Carnegie Corporation over the last ten years, the Project on East-West Relations, to which the issues considered in the pages that follow have been central. I appreciate the support of the Council's president, Leslie H. Gelb.

I received helpful comments on earlier versions of this book from Stanley Hoffmann and Richard H. Ullman.

THE DAWN OF PEACE IN EUROPE

Nicholas X. Rizopoulos offered valuable suggestions on matters of organization, style, and substance.

My greatest debt is to my wife, Anne Mandelbaum, whose matchless editorial skills have made *The Dawn of Peace in Europe* far clearer than it would otherwise have been and whose personal contributions would take another book to describe.

INTRODUCTION

This is a book about peace in Europe after the Cold War. During the four and one-half decades of East-West rivalry, the question at the heart of the book's subject was whether the military balance between the two opposing European military coalitions, one led by the United States, the other by the Soviet Union, was stable. In the wake of the Cold War, the central question is broader: How can and should Europe be organized politically and militarily to assure that the countries of the continent remain secure and at peace? The nine chapters that follow, which address that question, are divided into three parts, with three chapters in each part.

The first part concerns the future of the North Atlantic Treaty Organization. During the Cold War the Atlantic Alliance consisted of a roster of members with a common and clearly defined mission. It could retain both. The perpetuation of the status quo in NATO is the subject of chapter 1. Another possible future for the alliance, to which chapter 2 is devoted, is to retain its Cold War membership but change its mission to the assumption of responsibility for political and military problems outside its original geographic sphere of concern, as in Bosnia. A third possibility, the subject of chapter 3, is to retain the Cold War mission—deterring aggression from the East—but to expand the membership to include some of the countries of Central Europe that overthrew communism in 1989. In 1994, the current members of NATO committed themselves in principle to expansion of this kind.

Each chapter returns a verdict on the proposal in question. The status quo is both desirable and feasible. (Its feasibility is also discussed in chapter 9.) Out-of-area missions are desirable but not feasible. Expansion is feasible but not desirable.

The most desirable future, which is not part of the ongoing discussion about the future of European security, includes, but goes well beyond, perpetuating NATO in its Cold War form. This "common security order" replaces the grim imperatives of power politics with a system of international relations involving more extensive, explicit cooperation than the sovereign states of Europe have ever practiced. It is the subject of the book's second part.

Chapter 4 is a detour from the close consideration of current politics and policies to a more abstract level of analysis. It surveys some of the assumptions and findings of the academic study of international politics in order to put the measures that comprise common security into a perspective in which their significance can be appreciated—as a dramatic departure from past security arrangements in Europe that promises a more peaceful continent, at lower cost, than ever before.

A security order of this kind is plainly desirable. It is also feasible: A common security order has come into existence in post-Cold War Europe. Its core is the series of arms control accords signed between December 1987 and January 1993. Although similar in form to postwar arms treaties, they are different in content.

They have two distinguishing features. One, the subject of chapter 5, is "defense dominance." The treaties have reshaped the military balance in Europe to make armed forces more suitable for defending national territory but less so for seizing the territory of others. The other feature, discussed in chapter 6, is "transparency." Each country is obliged to make publicly available information about the size and the operations of its forces. Thus all countries can be confident that each is observing the agreements that all have signed and can know what every country is doing with the forces it is entitled, under the treaties, to have.

Because adherence is voluntary, the common security order is fragile. The two countries the participation of which is most in doubt are the subjects of the book's third part. They are the two that dominated the security affairs of the continent during the Cold War: Russia and the United States.

Chapter 7 addresses the future of domestic politics in Russia, exploring how the end of the Soviet Union, the collapse of the Communist political and economic systems, and the slow, unsteady beginnings of democratic politics and free markets are likely to affect Russia's commitment to the new security order. Chapter 8 discusses Russia's relations with its neighbors: those to the west, which are part of the European security order, and those to the south and east, where Russian policies are relevant to common security insofar as they affect what kind of country Russia becomes and how it conducts its policies toward its Western neighbors.

The conclusion of these two chapters is that the reasons to fear that Russia will overturn the institutions and practices of common security are no more powerful or compelling than the reasons to hope that, in the end, the new Russia will remain a good citizen of the new Europe.

The United States is integral to the common security order, as it is to each of the three different versions of NATO's future. Chapter 9 therefore returns to the subject of the first part of the book, assessing the durability of the American commitment to the Atlantic Alliance and therefore to a role in European security.

The three parts of *The Dawn of Peace in Europe* concern three different subjects, indeed three different *kinds* of subjects. The first addresses a series of current issues of public policy; the second has to do with concepts and ideas of interest to professional students of international politics; the third speculates about the future of the world's two greatest military powers. The three fit together as a single argument in the following way: NATO, the subject of part I, is necessary for a secure Europe in the post-Cold War era, but the two ambitious expansions of its Cold War role that have been proposed are unnecessary, because of the existence of a new common security order, which is described in part II. The durability of this new order depends on the continuing participation of Russia and the United States, the issues that part III considers.

Russia, the United States, and Germany are the countries that receive the most attention because they are the countries most important for the future of European security. The roles of two other historic great powers, Britain and France, remain important, but not as important. Because they will influence the international politics of Europe, domestic issues in Russia and the United States are the subjects of chapters 7 and 9. But these chapters do not examine in detail the ebb and flow of party politics or the details of particular elections in either country. What matters in Russia is the character of the regime, in the United States the structure of public opinion, although both factors will surely be influenced by the day-to-day politics of each country.

The Dawn of Peace in Europe describes and assesses five distinct, although not in each case mutually exclusive, futures for European security: three versions of NATO and two attempts to escape the traditional power politics of Europe—common security by reforming those politics and American isolation by removing from European politics the one country that is part of Europe as a matter of choice rather than geography.

Why are these, and not others, the options available? The array of choices is neither random nor accidental. None of the five is entirely new. Each is a late-twentieth-century version of policies that were proposed or tried during one of the three periods of modern European history comparable to the present: the aftermaths of the Napoleonic Wars and World Wars I and II.

After 1991, as after 1815, 1918, and 1945, a long, costly, dangerous European conflict has come to a decisive conclusion. Like Napoleonic France and Wilhelmine and Nazi Germany, the Soviet Union was defeated and reduced in size, and a government similar to those of the winners was installed on its territory. As in the other three conflicts, the conclusion of the Cold War brought to an end not simply a war but also an entire system of international relations in Europe, creating the need to construct a new one. Although less vividly than on previous occasions, the shadow of the recent past hangs over the deliberations about how to do so. Each of the five scenarios for European security provides an answer to the inevitable question: How can a recurrence of the conflict just concluded be avoided?

The withdrawal of the United States from Europe is not a plan for peace so much as a way for one country to avoid quarrels in which it believes it has no direct stake. American isolation would repeat the policy followed by Britain after 1815 and the United States after 1918. The two countries had involved themselves in Europe's wars temporarily, in a departure from their normal practice. They had intervened for the limited purpose of ensuring that a single, aggressive, imperial power did not subdue the entire continent, which it could then use as a base to threaten them directly. Once the would-be hegemonic power was defeated and a rough military equilibrium on the continent restored, the "offshore balancer," as the British thought of themselves, could bring its forces home.

As for common security, the search for some set of arrangements promising more durable peace than could be provided by the power politics that had dominated Europe's international relations, and had produced the four major wars, was a natural postwar development. The aspiration to transform international politics in order to prevent the terrible bloodshed to which it periodically gives rise was at its purest and most powerful after World War I. This was the brief, shining moment when the American president, Woodrow Wilson, lifted the spirits of a shattered continent with a vision of a peaceful world over which a new international organization—the League of Nations—would preside.

Ironically, these recurrent hopes were, if anything, more modest in the wake of the Cold War than after the two world wars, while the prospects for a more peaceful Europe were and are far brighter. Common security does not transform Europe in the way that Wilson had envisioned, however. It is closer in form to an earlier precedent: the Concert of Europe that followed the Napoleonic Wars.

The proposal to expand NATO eastward is in the tradition of recurrent postwar efforts to confine the defeated power within its new borders. The victors' strategy after the Napoleonic wars and World War I was to surround the defeated power, France and Germany respectively, with newly created buffer states, which were to serve as barriers to expansion and shock absorbers between the victors and the vanquished. In one sense this has already happened in the wake of the Cold War: The countries of Central and Eastern Europe were freed from Soviet-imposed Communist rule, and the former Soviet republics, having been liberated from the Soviet Union itself, are now independent countries. They are the buffer between Russia and the easternmost member of the winning coalition, Germany. The purpose of bringing some of them into NATO is to strengthen that buffer.

The enthusiasm for out-of-area missions for NATO represents the revival of another characteristic project of postwar periods: the organization by the winning coalition of a kind of standing police force. The proposals for a Holy Alliance after the Napoleonic Wars, for a strong Council of the League of Nations to which the great powers would belong after World War I, for Franklin Roosevelt's four policemen—the United States, Great Britain, the Soviet Union, and China—during World War II and the designation of a United Nations Security Council afterward, were all intended to deal with smaller conflicts that could, if unchecked, lead to larger wars such as the one just concluded. The combined efforts of the strongest powers would, it was hoped, stamp out brush fires before they turned into all-consuming conflagrations.*

The Europe-wide interest in sustaining NATO in its Cold War form echoes efforts after the three previous conflicts, especially after World War I, to keep the winning coalition together. The purpose was to hedge against the possibility that the power just defeated—France in the first case, Germany in the second and third—would rise again to threaten Europe. The reason for perpetuating NATO is to provide insurance against a neoimperial Russian foreign policy to the west.

The parallels with comparable historical moments make clear how much has changed in Europe in a few years and how much more fluid the international relations of the continent became with the ending of the Cold War. The range of possibilities for European security has abruptly and dramatically broadened. During the Cold War, when the politics of Europe were frozen, security questions were military

---

*The post-Cold War motives were as much humanitarian as strategic. The purpose was to save lives in countries where fighting was taking place rather than to protect the interests of the nations contributing to the police force. That is one of the reasons that the idea attracted little support. See chapter 2.

in character. In the wake of the conflict, as after the previous great wars, the most important considerations are political.

The comparisons with the previous postwar eras demonstrate as well, however, that while the range of possibilities is wider, it is not infinitely wide. Certain issues, and certain responses to them, recur. That is the reason the historical parallels are so striking.

For European security, therefore, the past is relevant to the future. It is not an infallible guide: History does not faithfully repeat itself. What happened to the historical antecedents of the five futures for European security described in the pages that follow does, however, help to illuminate the advantages, disadvantages, and obstacles associated with the late-twentieth-century avatars of these patterns of the past.

Although the problem of European security is dramatically different in the post-Cold War era than it was during the Cold War, the two periods share one principal feature: the central importance of the Atlantic Alliance. The status and the future of NATO, therefore, is the starting point of *The Dawn of Peace in Europe*.

~Part I~
NATO's Future

~1~

THE STATUS QUO

The North Atlantic Treaty Organization is the most successful military alliance in history. For more than four decades of confrontation with a powerful, nuclear-armed adversary it held together a multinational coalition composed of markedly different countries, some recently bitter enemies, the most powerful of them separated from the others by 3,500 miles of ocean. It won a sweeping victory without firing a shot.

That victory, however, liquidated the circumstances under which NATO was born and flourished. The Soviet power in Europe that it was created to contain is gone. The ideology of Marxism-Leninism, which made Soviet power particularly dangerous by endowing it with a messianic mission, is dead. The Soviet Union itself, the driving force behind both the power and the ideology that NATO was called into being to oppose, has disintegrated.

The principal Soviet successor state, Russia, has abandoned the ideology and lost much of the military power of the Soviet Union. Russia's military forces, such as they are, are now separated from Germany, the defense of which was NATO's central Cold War military mission, by almost 1,000 miles and two sovereign states—Poland and Ukraine—neither of them aligned with Russia.

Like other military alliances, NATO was created in response to a threat. That threat is now gone. Yet the future of NATO remains of intense interest. Why is this so?

Lord Ismay, NATO's first secretary-general, memorably described the alliance's threefold purpose as being "to keep the Americans in, the Russians out, and the Germans down." The fascination with the future of NATO lies in the fact that those three purposes remain relevant for Europe's governments, despite the momentous changes the end of the Cold War has brought.

Ismay's first two purposes were, of course, NATO's explicit aims. An alliance is formed to oppose an adversary, in this case the Soviet Union. The Atlantic Alliance was designed to include the United States, the presence of which was deemed essential because in 1949 the countries of Western Europe seemed too weak to counterbalance Soviet power. One reason for their relative weakness was that when NATO was founded the military might of the potentially strongest Western European country, Germany, was unavailable. The war had devastated Germany militarily and discredited it politically.

Ismay's phrase is often cited not only because it is pithy but also because of the third purpose it expresses. NATO was designed to address not only the next European war but also the last one. The alliance sought to keep the Soviet Union at arm's length and Germany in a tight embrace, thus protecting Western Europe from both. It was American membership that made it possible to do both simultaneously; the American presence in Europe enabled NATO to be the instrument of "double containment."[1]

This third purpose bears emphasizing because, by the end of the Cold War, it had become the most obscure and least discussed of the alliance's original aims, yet it remained a major consideration in the politics of post-Cold War European security. NATO was part of the solution to what came to be known, in the twentieth century, as the German problem. German power and ambition, and Europe's inability to deal with them, had disturbed the peace of the continent and the world for 75 years between Prussia's victory over France in 1871 and Hitler's final defeat in 1945. The German problem was the precipitating cause of the two world wars. Germany's neighbors were unable or unwilling to agree on a role for Germany that was acceptable to the Germans themselves.

After World War II the Germany of the Third Reich was reduced in size, its eastern provinces ceded to Poland and the Soviet Union. It was also divided into two separate states, with each occupied by a part of the coalition that had defeated Hitler. Western troops protected the German Federal Republic, which had a legitimate democratic government, against threats from the armies of the Warsaw Treaty Organization. Communist, mainly Soviet, troops guarded the rulers of the German Democratic Republic against internal challenges from the people they governed. This combination ensured that neither East nor West Germany could threaten the peace of Europe.[2]

In addition to dividing Germany and occupying part of it, the Western powers offered a third response to the German problem, which turned out to be more important than the other two: West Germany was admitted to membership in what became a political and economic community of democratic, market-oriented countries on both sides of the Atlantic.* Because this last response was so successful, Ismay's third purpose became all but unmentionable, at least explicitly. Because NATO's other members treated the German Federal Republic as a full and respected member of the community of Western democracies, which it was, it bordered on the offensive openly to voice distrust of the Germans.

To be sure, that distrust diminished sharply over time. West Germany's forty-year history of democratic, peaceful behavior and its immersion in the multilateral institutions of the global and Western community made the task of keeping Germany down a far less urgent one than it had seemed in the second half of the 1940s, when the world was embarking on the long, expensive recovery from the terrible physical and moral destruction wrought by the Third Reich.

Still, distrust of Germany did not entirely disappear. It was on display in 1989 and 1990 when, in the wake of the opening of the Berlin Wall, the two German states moved toward unification. The leaders of two of West Germany's closest allies, President François Mitterrand of France and Prime Minister Margaret Thatcher of Great Britain, made clear their doubts about the wisdom of permitting the formation of a single German state. Neither was powerful or determined enough to block unification; but each expressed the persisting fear that a larger, more independent Germany would cause trouble in Europe.

---

* Along with NATO itself, the principal institutional vehicle for integrating Germany into the Western community, indeed for creating that community, was the European Common Market. It began in 1950 as the European Coal and Steel Community, a scheme for limited economic cooperation between France and Germany. Over the years its membership expanded and its economic integration deepened. It became the European Common Market, then the European Community, then the European Union. Its founding purpose, to contain Germany, was an important motive for each step forward, including the Maastricht Treaty of 1991. A major theme of the postwar history of Western Europe is thus the embrace of Germany by its friends and neighbors in order to contain it.

In the eyes of the governments that belong to the Atlantic Alliance, moreover, the other two founding purposes that Lord Ismay listed remain valid. The same kinds of doubts that its recent adversaries harbored about Germany in the wake of World War II envelop Russia in the wake of the Cold War. The country's future is uncertain. The resumption of an aggressive, imperial Russian foreign policy cannot be ruled out.

There is thus a consensus in the West that the perpetuation of NATO in some form is desirable. It is still important to keep an eye on the Russians and a hand—friendly, but firm—on the Germans. For these two purposes an American commitment to Europe is indispensable.

Because Germany is a trusted ally and Russia no longer an officially designated adversary, this cannot be said directly. But it is said indirectly. In November 1991, NATO convened a summit meeting in Rome to produce something that was plainly necessary in light of the collapse of communism in Europe: a fresh strategic concept. The document that emerged presented four security functions for the alliance. Advertised as new, they were in fact versions of Ismay's old, familiar purposes.

The first, "to provide one of the indispensable foundations for a stable security environment in Europe,"[3] was a general argument for leaving NATO in place as a hedge against uncertainty. The next three points were arguments in favor of keeping the Americans in, the Russians out, and the Germans down.

The second function, "to serve . . . as a transatlantic forum for allied consultations," referred to the need to keep the United States actively involved in European affairs. The third, "to deter and defend any threat of aggression against the territory of any NATO member state," alluded to the possibility of a resurgence of Russian imperial behavior. The fourth new function, "to preserve the strategic balance within Europe," referred obliquely to Germany. Europe in this case meant *Western* Europe. Without the United States, the balance of political power there would tilt sharply toward its largest, richest country—Germany; and whatever Western military and political structure remained would inevitably have a large German component.

The search for insurance against a resurgent Russia is the post-Cold War version of the recurrent and understandable impulse, in the wake of a major European war, to hedge against a renewed threat from the defeated power. Like France after 1815 and Germany after 1918 and 1945, Russia remains potentially the strongest power on the European continent. In nuclear weaponry it is the strongest power. Like France and Germany before it, although Russia's military power has collapsed, its borders have contracted, and the government in power during the conflict has been overthrown, its imperial aspirations have not necessarily been extinguished for all time. Like Napoleonic France and Wilhelmine and Nazi Germany, the Soviet Union was defeated only with the assistance of an offshore power: Britain in the first instance, Britain allied with the United States in the next three. After the Cold War, as after the previous great European wars, keeping the winning coalition together seemed only prudent.

A distinctive feature of the conflict with the Soviet Union and of the post-Cold War era provides an additional incentive for sustaining that coalition in some form: nuclear weapons. The bomb is the great geopolitical trump card; and for all the humiliation it has suffered, for all its weakness, Russia retains a large and powerful nuclear arsenal.

This means that countries that share the European continent with Russia need some means of counterbalancing Russian nuclear might; without this, in any dispute that might arise Russia would have a potentially decisive advantage. During the Cold War the United States assumed responsibility for nuclear balancing. While Britain and France also acquired nuclear weapons, it was

the American arsenal, not theirs, upon which the nonnuclear countries of Western Europe, in particular Germany,
relied for protection.

In the post-Cold War era the United States retains that
role by custom and habit as well as by treaty. The distribution of nuclear weapons is heavily regulated, and the regu-
lations—enumerated in arms treaties—designate the United
States as the main Western custodian of nuclear firepower.[4]
To be sure, there is no technical obstacle to the Europeans
themselves assuming all of the responsibility for their own
nuclear protection. The obstacle, rather, is political and has
to do with Ismay's third purpose.

The withdrawal of the United States from Europe
would lead to a more powerful Germany. Without
American forces, the Europeans would have to provide
their own defense. In that case, Germany might well calcu-
late, as it did during the Cold War, that British and French
nuclear weapons afforded it insufficient protection,* and
seek to acquire its own nuclear weapons.

Perhaps this would not happen. Perhaps, with the end
of the Cold War, if the United States withdrew its nuclear
umbrella from Germany the Germans would deem the
nuclear protection they could get from Britain and France to
be adequate.[5] But even the Germans themselves could not
be certain what they would decide to do under such circumstances. They might, to the contrary, conclude that
Europe had become a more dangerous place, that they

---

* The assumption that French and British nuclear weapons protected only
the countries that possessed them and not other Western European countries had a practical effect on arms control negotiations with the Soviet
Union. The United States successfully excluded British and French armaments from the negotiations during the 1970s and 1980s on the not always
explicitly stated grounds that Soviet nuclear weapons threatened Germany
but French and British forces did not protect the Federal Republic. The
excluded French and British nuclear weapons did, however, threaten the
Soviet Union.

could not rely on others to protect them, and that they therefore needed a nuclear arsenal of their own. The structure of
the Atlantic Alliance shielded Germany and Europe from
that decision. This is one of the reasons that, during the Cold
War, the consensus in favor of NATO was so broad and deep.
It was especially powerful among the Germans themselves,
who did not wish to be put in a position in which they would
feel obliged to consider the nuclear option seriously. To per-
petuate the NATO status quo into the post-Cold War era is a
way of continuing to relieve Germany of the opportunity—or
the obligation—to contemplate such a course.

On this central post-Cold War issue the international
discussion takes place in code, in order to avoid raising suspicions about a close and valued ally, and in the case of the
Germans themselves to avoid speaking openly about the
fears that others have about them and that Germans themselves may partly share. The status quo is desirable, it is
said, to avoid the "renationalization" of European defense.
The country for which an independent national military
force and security policy is thought undesirable is not Spain
or Norway. Nor is it France, for which, after Charles de
Gaulle withdrew from NATO's integrated military command in 1965, the *nationalization* of defense policy became a
cardinal principle of foreign policy.

Anxiety about the renationalization of European security policy, that is, of a politically independent, militarily
powerful Germany, was the reason for Mitterrand and
Thatcher's reservations about German reunification. When
their reservations were overridden by the Americans and
the Germans, they and the other Europeans fell back on the
need to sustain NATO in some form, in order to "keep
Germany down." For this reason all the countries of Europe,
including not only Germany but also Russia, which acquiesced in membership in the alliance for a united Germany,
favor the continuation of NATO's basic arrangements.[6]
NATO's status quo, or more accurately, because Cold War

force levels are not being sustained, status quo minus, pro-
vokes no opposition among the governments of Europe and
North America.

It is scarcely imaginable that a reunified Germany, freed
from the restraints of the Cold War era, would run amok,
launching another campaign of imperial conquest in Europe,
nor does any Western government believe that it would. The
German Federal Republic remains stable, democratic, and
not only peace-loving but also emphatically conflict-averse,
opposed to having its own nuclear weapons and to anything
other than a purely defensive German military role.

Under changed circumstances, however, German wishes might not be a reliable guide to German policy. Shorn of
American protection, Germany might prefer not to increase
its military power but nonetheless feel compelled to do so
for its own safety. This would lead to a new and unknown—
or, alternatively, all too well known—situation: a powerful,
independent Germany. Europe lived dangerously with a
large, independent Germany for seven decades; and then
comfortably with a reduced, confined, divided Germany
for the better part of an additional five.

The continuation of the status quo for NATO is thus a
form of insurance not only against Russia but also against a
Germany compelled to conduct an independent security
policy. It is insurance that the Germans themselves want.
They understand that their neighbors will be confident that
they are committed to international good citizenship to the
extent that they are firmly anchored in the Atlantic Alliance.
The commitment to NATO is thus a self-denying ordinance
that Germany has enthusiastically embraced and for which
it is happy to pay.

During the Cold War, NATO was an instrument of double containment. It contained the Soviet Union overtly while
also quietly containing one of its own members, Germany.
The governments of Europe want something like this double containment to continue into the post-Cold War era. But

they do not, and can not, want the continuation of NATO's precise Cold War role: There is nothing—no country—to be contained in the Cold War sense of the term.

Containment connotes an active threat. Germany actively threatens none of its neighbors and, barring an unforeseen cataclysm, will threaten none of them. Nor does Russia credibly threaten its neighbors to the west. It would not require a cataclysm for Russia to mount such a threat, but five years after the collapse of the Soviet Union this had not taken place.[7]

What the governments of Europe therefore believe they need is not military preparations to deter a mobilized adversary, as during the Cold War, but instead a response to uncertainty. The immediate danger in post-Cold War Europe is not aggression but rather the rise of circumstances out of which aggression might ultimately emerge. It is a danger at one remove: The response required is not deterrence per se but a measure of assurance that new threats are unlikely to arise and will be resisted if they do. The historian and strategist Michael Howard has drawn a distinction that is relevant here, between deterrence and what he calls "reassurance," which he defines as policies and measures that instill confidence in allies so that they can conduct their domestic affairs and foreign policies without feeling intimidated.[8]

In Europe, an American military presence provides reassurance by serving as a buffer between and among countries that are at peace but nonetheless harbor residual suspicions of one another. Although not adversaries in the post-Cold War era, they have been adversaries in the past and can imagine, without resorting to scenarios lifted from the pages of science fiction novels, circumstances in which they would be adversaries in the future. The American presence is a barrier against the creation of such circumstances.

The United States plays an analogous military role in the Asia-Pacific region. There, relations between Japan and

China correspond to the relationship, in Europe, between Germany and Russia. During the Cold War, the two pairs of countries were adversaries. In each case one was protected and the other opposed by the United States. With the end of the Cold War (in the case of Japan and China, before the conflict with the Soviet Union in Europe ended), the military and political rivalry eased.

A residue of distrust remains, however, the legacy of a history of bitter animosity and war. Russia and China further inspire at least muted suspicion because of their nuclear arsenals and their sheer size, and because, even though the two have abandoned orthodox Marxism-Leninism, strong currents of nationalism are part of their politics, which in neither case is fully democratic.[9] The American military forces assigned to Europe and the Asia-Pacific region reassure Germany and Japan, respectively, that they are protected against both residual and potential threats from their two large neighbors.

At the same time, the American presence reassures Russia and China that neither Germany nor Japan will be tempted to increase its military forces sharply, add nuclear weapons to them, or adopt substantially different security policies. If the most powerful countries of Asia and Europe are reassured about each other, their less powerful neighbors, in East and Southeast Asia and in Central and Western Europe, will themselves be reassured.

In Europe, the continuation of NATO in its Cold War form, if not necessarily at its Cold War strength, is a way of assuring all interested parties that the military status quo there, and thus the geopolitical status quo, will not change suddenly or dramatically. That message is reassuring because the post-Cold War status quo is, for the moment, satisfactory to all, or at least preferable to any likely alternative.

Thus reassurance is the purpose of perpetuating NATO, a quintessentially Cold War institution, into the post-Cold War era, and, like Monsieur Jourdain in Moliere's play *The*

Bourgeois Gentleman, who discovered that he had been speaking prose all his life, the Atlantic Alliance is already practicing reassurance. The American connection to Europe through NATO helps to create a sense of confidence that the military and political conditions in which Europeans live are stable.[10]

Reassurance is, in fact, easier to practice than to describe. No authoritative statement of the new mission has been offered. Even if such a statement existed, it would not provide the basis for answering the most fundamental of military questions: How much is enough? The answer is ordinarily based on the size and strength of the military establishment that the force in question is being assembled to oppose. What the policy of reassurance is designed to address—uncertainty—does not provide a useful yardstick against which to judge the adequacy of an army, a navy, an air force, or a nuclear arsenal.

If reassurance is easier to practice than to describe, moreover, it is easier to describe than to justify. In fact, virtually no effort has been made to justify it, in part, no doubt, because of the anticipated skepticism of the Western publics. The shift from deterrence to reassurance presents an even more formidable task than military planning—that of domestic political management.

The policy of deterrence commanded robust support on both sides of the Atlantic for four decades. It was plausible, familiar, and compelling; it was the international version of an emergency, a way of coping with an obvious danger. Reassurance involves far less clarity and responds to no immediate danger. It is counterintuitive. While in the late 1940s establishing an alliance to "keep Germany down" was a prudent hedge against a plausible threat, fifty years later perpetuating that alliance for the same purpose is more likely to be seen as an act of unwarranted distrust of a close, loyal ally. Furthermore, insofar as NATO is a mechanism for the United States to defend

Germany, Americans are bound to notice that the country is not visibly threatened and in any event is rich enough to defend itself.

Nor does reassurance have a well-known historical antecedent, as did deterrence, which was portrayed and seen as a way to avoid a huge, destructive war like the one fought against Hitler. Moreover, reassurance, even if it can be made to seem a worthy goal, does not seem automatically to require the creation and maintenance of expensive armed forces. Deterrence is part of the language of strategy. Reassurance is a concept more familiar in psychology.

Doubts about reassurance are thought to be strongest in the American public, which has become the weak link in NATO. The slogan "Yankee go home" is seen nowhere in Europe in the wake of the Cold War; but "Yankee *come* home" has a certain resonance on the western side of the Atlantic—or so Europeans fear. For four decades Americans were willing to pay for the forces necessary to stop a westward thrust by Soviet tanks on the north German plain. Whether they will be willing to pay—to pay less, to be sure, but to pay something—to ease Europe's anxieties about Germany, a wealthy, democratic ally, or to ease the Germans' anxieties about themselves remains to be seen.[11]

The foremost champions of continuing the alliance, the officials charged with conducting the foreign policies of its existing members, are not fully confident that the American public will agree to underwrite NATO in the post-Cold War era. Organizations can and do outlive the circumstances in which they are founded, but they do not usually survive for long if they serve no discernible or necessary purpose.

Thus, in addition to the fear of the revival in some form of the German foreign policy of the period between the world wars, there is another unvoiced anxiety that is part of the subdued, sometimes coded discussion about the perpetuation of NATO: anxiety about the return of the American policy of that period, a policy of withdrawing from Europe's political affairs. Keeping the Americans in remains a prerequisite for keeping the Russians out and the Germans down. But the new mission of reassurance, no matter how important, may not suffice to assure the continuing engagement of the United States in Europe, or so it is feared.[12]

It is these concerns, about NATO's capacity to perform the task on which all agree, that partly accounts for the post-Cold War interest in giving it other tasks, one of which involves the active use of what NATO has specialized in providing: armed forces.

While Europe does not lack for opportunities for using armed forces, the opportunities are located not at the heart of the continent but on its periphery, outside NATO's designated area of responsibility. They call, moreover, for actions other than waging the major combined-arms war for which the Atlantic Alliance prepared for four decades. These are opportunities that not only provide a rationale for perpetuating NATO but also involve the alliance in addressing problems that seem worth solving in their own right.

These are out-of-area missions. The proponents of intervention in the test case, Bosnia, argued on both humanitarian and strategic grounds that NATO action was justified. But a tacit rationale for the NATO operations there was the hope of putting the alliance on a firm footing in public opinion in the post-Cold War era, a hope captured in the words of one of the advocates of such missions, Senator Richard Lugar of Indiana: "out of area or out of business."[13]

~2~

OUT-OF-AREA MISSIONS

What was, during the Cold War, NATO's principal military front is no longer the site of a confrontation. Germany has become a united, democratic member of the Atlantic Alliance rather than a country divided between two governments and two military blocs in which two powerful opposing armies are deployed. Other parts of Europe, however, are more turbulent than during the Cold War. The post-Cold War era has proven to be politically disorderly, creating the need for a mechanism to impose order. Because it pools the resources and the experience of powerful democracies and because it is well endowed with the instruments of order—military forces—NATO has been nominated to be that mechanism.

It has been nominated by, among others, the German defense minister Volker Ruehe, who called on the alliance to adopt a "comprehensive crisis management strategy."[1] The crises that have needed managing have appeared on the periphery of Europe, beyond the area for which NATO assumed responsibility for more than four decades. An out-of-area mission would have the added benefit, its proponents believe, of giving the Western publics, on whose support the alliance depends for its continuing existence, a new reason to provide that support. A NATO prepared to keep order on Europe's periphery would be an organization ready to address the problems of the present and the future rather than simply those of the past.

Previous periods following great European wars spawned similar proposals: The Austrian foreign minister Clemens von Metternich's idea for a Holy Alliance after the Napoleonic Wars was designed to stamp out stirrings of nationalism in Europe of the kind the French Revolution had unleashed and that threatened the thrones of dynasties such as the Habsburgs, which Metternich served. The Council of Woodrow Wilson's League of Nations after World War I was to take responsibility for quelling instability. Franklin Roosevelt envisioned "Four Policemen"—the United States, the Soviet Union, Great Britain, and China—that would patrol the world after World War II. The idea foreshadowed the designation of five countries—Roosevelt's four plus France—as permanent members of the United Nations Security Council. Each of these ideas was a proposal for an international police force to keep order in Europe and beyond. Each assumed that the victorious coalition could continue into the postwar era as a kind of permanent posse, to stop or punish violations of international norms.

All failed. Each time, the underlying assumption—that the victorious powers could agree both on the desirable norms for the postwar world and on the importance of enforcing them—proved mistaken. The members of the winning coalition were never of one mind about the rules that the proposed multinational posse would enforce. The British, for example, refused to be part of Metternich's Holy

Alliance. While they were willing to help suppress international aggression that could threaten them, they would not contribute to the repression of the forces of nationalism or liberalism wherever they appeared on the European continent. Even when the members of the winning coalition could agree on what ought to be done, they were not always prepared to contribute to getting it done. They had been willing to make common cause to prevent one great power from dominating the others, but were generally unwilling to do so to settle lesser quarrels or to subdue minor uprisings.

The post-Cold War era at first seemed more promising in this regard. It began with a successful demonstration of international cooperation to reverse a blatant transgression and punish the transgressor: the Persian Gulf conflict of 1990–91. When Saddam Hussein's forces invaded and occupied Kuwait, a large, powerful international coalition assembled to confront, attack, and evict them. Operations "Desert Shield" and "Desert Storm" were textbook examples of international police work: An outlaw went on a rampage, a posse formed to pursue him, order was restored, and justice done. In his inaugural address Bill Clinton, whose presidency was the first to take place entirely in the post-Cold War era, suggested that a precedent had been set: When "the will and conscience of the international community are defied," he said, "we will act, with peaceful diplomacy wherever possible, with force when necessary."

The Gulf War was not formally a NATO operation. The anti-Saddam coalition received contributions, in money and armed forces, from many countries outside the Atlantic Alliance; but NATO members nonetheless played crucial roles in the war, and the army that liberated Kuwait was drawn heavily from the ranks of the forces permanently stationed in Germany to deter an attack by the Warsaw Pact.[2]

The campaign to evict Iraq from Kuwait succeeded because the episode had several important features that are unlikely to be present elsewhere. First, a vital international interest was at stake: oil. Had Saddam Hussein not met the opposition he did, he would have consolidated control of Kuwait and exercised powerful influence over neighboring Saudi Arabia. In that case he would have held sway over 40 percent of the world's known oil reserves, which would have given him enormous power in the region and beyond.[3]

Second, the United States took the lead both in assembling the coalition and in fighting the war. Although many countries made contributions of some kind, most of the combat power brought to bear on the Iraqi forces was American.

Finally, the Persian Gulf war was a familiar type of military operation. It was the kind of mission for which NATO had prepared for decades, indeed for which armed forces have always prepared: to fight and win a war. The equipment that had been purchased and the skills developed for Europe proved effective in the Gulf.

Saddam had defied the world's "conscience"; the Iraqi invasion and occupation of Kuwait was a clear, universally acknowledged violation of international law. The international community responded decisively because a large common interest was in jeopardy: the control of much of the world's oil reserves.[4] With the passage of time, however, the Persian Gulf war has appeared less the prototypical post-Cold War conflict. The more representative opportunity for Ruehe's "comprehensive crisis management," one in which NATO became officially involved as an alliance and ultimately did intervene for the purpose of making peace, came in the Balkans.

Bosnia was the site of the alliance's most serious engagement outside the borders of its member states in the wake of the Cold War. It is the place, in fact, where NATO first saw combat as an alliance. NATO played several roles while the conflict among Serbs, Croats, and Muslims was under way, beginning in 1992.

It helped to enforce a United Nations-decreed embargo on Serbia: Ships assigned to NATO patrolled the Adriatic coast. NATO warplanes patrolled a "no-fly" zone, also decreed by the UN, over Bosnia. NATO air power was also placed at the service of enforcing "exclusion zones," also known as "safe areas," that the UN had proclaimed around several besieged cities in eastern Bosnia. In the late summer of 1995 that mission expanded to a more general air campaign against Serb military positions in Bosnia. Two NATO members, Britain and France, put their own troops on the ground in Bosnia, but as peacekeepers under UN auspices rather than as combatants in a NATO military operation. At the end of 1995, the NATO military presence was vastly expanded. The alliance assumed responsibility for monitoring and enforcing a settlement to which the warring parties had finally agreed, and dispatched 60,000 troops, 20,000 of which were American, to the former Yugoslav republic for this purpose.

The NATO role in Bosnia is unlikely, however, to serve as a precedent for other out-of-area commitments. NATO's Bosnian intervention was hesitant, reluctant, limited, and only modestly successful in reaching the goals that at least some members had initially sought to achieve. Moreover, in the United States the Bosnia operation was unpopular. There was no consensus within NATO on either the proper settlement in Bosnia or on the importance of ending the fighting on any terms. Nor was a consensus on either point likely to be any firmer for other conflicts elsewhere in Europe, Eurasia, or beyond. Whatever NATO was able to accomplish in Bosnia, it was likely to achieve less elsewhere.

Several features particular to the Bosnian conflict complicated NATO's role there. In the period leading up to the war, which was when the cost of containing it was lowest, the members of the alliance were preoccupied with matters more important to them: the Persian Gulf war and the

ongoing disintegration of the Soviet Union. Little high-level
NATO attention was available for a conflict in the Balkans.

When Yugoslavia began to disintegrate, Western Europe
assumed it could cope with the consequences there without American help. The European Union took initial responsibility for preventing, then containing and trying to stop,
the wars that erupted. The other international organization
that early on was drawn into Yugoslavia was the United
Nations. The American government took the position that
the United States would not, and NATO should not, become
involved.[5] The reasons for the alliance's hesitation over
Bosnia, however, go beyond the simultaneous appearance
of other international problems and the primacy at first
accorded other international organizations.

NATO's members came to the conflicts in Yugoslavia
with different sympathies, which had their roots in history
and domestic politics. The Germans championed the cause
of Croatian independence, and, at the outset of 1992, pres-
sured the European Union to recognize the Croatian secession from Yugoslavia. They did so not because Croatia had
been an ally of the Third Reich during World War II, but
rather because, as a Catholic country with émigrés residing
in Germany, Croatia evoked sympathy from the German
public, especially in Catholic Bavaria.

In the United States, the Clinton administration became
convinced that the Muslim-dominated government of
Bosnia had been the victim of international aggression. The
administration decided that important principles of international law as well as substantial American interests were
at stake in Bosnia's struggle to survive and to control the
territory that the Bosnian republic of Yugoslavia had encompassed.

Britain and France, by contrast, were better disposed
toward the Serbs. Neither condoned the ethnic cleansing of
which the Serbs were the most extensive, although not the
only, practitioners; but memories of the Serbs' anti-fascist

stand in World War II were alive in both countries. More importantly, the two governments believed that stability in the Balkans required that the Serbs, the region's most numerous group, receive some satisfaction of their national claims. Although giving no direct military support to them, the Russian government also sympathized with the Serbs, whose cause, although not a matter of great importance to Russia, evoked a measure of sympathy for fellow Orthodox Slavs.

These different sympathies inevitably led to different interpretations of the conflict. For the American government, the war in Bosnia was a clear case of Serb aggression against the internationally recognized sovereign state of Bosnia, a position with which the Germans tended to agree. For Russia, the Serbs were fighting for self-determination. For Britain and France, the Bosnian conflict was an ugly, messy civil war among three parties none of which had a monopoly on either virtue or villainy, in a province that had never been fully self-governing but always part of a larger political unit and should therefore never have been recognized as an independent country.

Because their analyses of the conflict differed, the goals of the outside powers differed as well. The United States, especially after 1993 when the Clinton administration took office, wanted the Muslim-dominated Bosnian government based in Sarajevo to win the war—that is, to gain control over the entire territory of the former Yugoslav republic of Bosnia-Herzegovina. The American administration also wanted to punish the Serb perpetrators of war crimes against Muslims and sponsored the establishment of an international war crimes tribunal for the former Yugoslavia.

For Russia, the best outcome was the achievement of what the Serbs had sought: the secession of the Serb-controlled parts of Bosnia and their affiliation, in some manner, with Serbia.

Britain and France were willing to countenance some version of "greater Serbia." They were less concerned with achieving any particular outcome than with stopping the fighting. What they considered the greatest threat to their interests was not the reduction in size, or even the disappearance, of Bosnia. It was, rather, the continuation of the killings and the expulsions, mainly of Bosnian Muslims, from the former Yugoslavia, swelling the flow of refugees to Western Europe and risking the spread of the war to other parts of the Balkans. The troops London and Paris sent to Bosnia under UN auspices had the mission of protecting civilians, not of taking sides in the conflict. The UN sought to regulate the way the war was being fought while trying to negotiate its end.*

Perhaps the ultimate reason that it was difficult for the outside powers, including the principal members of NATO, to arrive at a consensus on the desirable outcome of the Bosnian conflict was that it pitted two internationally recognized principles of legitimacy against each other: the right to national self-determination, claimed by Bosnia's Serbs, and the sanctity of existing borders, asserted by Bosnia's Muslim-dominated government. To complicate matters further, while the United States and Germany insisted on defending the existing borders of Bosnia, they had been willing to ignore borders in the case of Yugoslavia, an internationally recognized country for seventy-five years, the collapse of which they had accepted, indeed helped to foster. The Western powers had not only recognized Croatia and Bosnia, but had also failed to make their recognition conditional on credible assurances that the governments of the new countries would respect the rights of those—mainly

---

*Although roundly criticized, especially in the United States, the UN mission did achieve a measure of success. It made possible a continuing supply of food to, and some protection for, Muslim civilians in Bosnian cities that were besieged by the Serbs, thus saving many lives.

Serbs—who had suddenly become national minorities within Croatia and Bosnia.

For all their differences, the Bosnia policies of the NATO members did share one central feature: For each the conflict there was, in the end, of minor importance, and so failed to meet a basic requirement of collective action such as the alliance's Cold War mission and the Persian Gulf war. Neither the Europeans nor the Americans were ever willing to invest their most precious commodity—the lives of their own soldiers—to affect the conflict decisively. Even the most ardent American champions of the cause of the Bosnian Muslims never suggested that the United States send ground troops to help them, claiming instead that air power alone could tilt the war in their favor.[6] During the war British and French troops were explicitly not sent to Bosnia to fight, and the 60,000-person NATO contingent dispatched there at the end of 1995 had the mission of enforcing a peace treaty to which the warring parties had agreed, rather than intervening in the war.

If one reason the alliance failed to act early and decisively in Bosnia was that its members disagreed on what they wanted to accomplish there, another was that all *did* agree that whatever they wanted was not worth a high price to obtain. On the other hand, the NATO allies believed, or felt, that *something* should be done, that the international community should not stand idly by and do nothing. They therefore designated the United Nations, by default, to act for them in Bosnia. The UN was authorized to perform the one task on which all could agree: the humanitarian mission of protecting civilians. The result of its efforts, however, was to erode international confidence in the UN itself. The civilians it was dispatched to protect were threatened by an ongoing war. Stopping the war required a political settlement. But there was no settlement because the warring sides, by definition, could not agree on one, and neither could the international community, which, even if it had

been of one mind on a settlement, was not willing to intervene forcefully to impose it. The UN was certainly not in a
position to impose anything, and yet became the object of
criticism for failing to do what it had neither the power nor
the authority to do. The severest criticism came from com-
mentators in, and officials of, the United States, a country
with the resources but without the will for this task.* The
UN thus began as a fig leaf and ended as a scapegoat for the
failures of individual governments, failures stemming from
the fact that the most powerful among them shared neither
a common goal in Bosnia nor the common belief that it was
vital to achieve any particular goal there.

NATO's difficulties in Bosnia stand in contrast to its
record during the Cold War. To be sure, the decades of confrontation with the Soviet Union were not free of intra-
alliance strife: Discord is normal even within an alliance.
When allies have an overriding common purpose, however—
opposing a major adversary—they put aside their differences. During the Cold War, NATO members agreed on the
need to contain the Soviet Union, although not always on
how best to do so and almost never on how to apportion
the costs of containment.

Moreover, unlike Bosnia, the NATO allies were persuaded that the goal of containing the Soviet Union, despite
their disagreements about apportioning its costs, was

---

*From 1993 onward the United States periodically pressed for the United
Nations to authorize bombing in support of the Bosnian government. UN
officials resisted because this would have jeopardized the safety of the
peacekeepers that a number of countries—not including the United States—
had agreed to send to Bosnia. A condition of dispatching these forces was
the promise by the UN, tacit or explicit, that they would not be put in
harm's way. A significant bombing campaign was finally authorized at the
end of August 1995. Because of the fall to the Serbs of the designated
Muslim "safe areas" that some countries, including the United States, had
insisted, over UN objections, that the UN peacekeepers protect, the peacekeepers were no longer vulnerable to Serb attacks or hostage-taking.

important enough to pay a high price to achieve. Over the course of forty years they devoted considerable resources to maintaining powerful military forces at the center of Europe. Behind those forces stood a firm commitment to use them, with the enormous costs that that would entail, to block a Soviet attack. From 1992 through the middle of 1995, Britain, France, the United States, and Germany were not willing to make the kind of effort necessary to stop the fighting in Bosnia because stopping the fighting was not crucial for any of them.

In the last quarter of 1995 the fighting did stop, after the bombing of Serb positions, American-led diplomacy, the Dayton peace accords and the dispatch of 60,000 NATO troops to enforce them. But even this concerted multinational effort did not fulfill the requirements for successful collective action.

The Americans and the Western Europeans compromised on their differing goals for Bosnia by forging a settlement that embraced both. The Dayton accords were a plan for partition, which the French and the British had been willing to accept from the beginning of the war. The accords divided Bosnia into two territorial units the borders of which corresponded roughly to the existing battle lines. One was a Serb republic, the other nominally combined Croats and Muslims but in practice the two were separate. Each entity had the right to affiliate with other countries: the Croat-Muslim federation with Croatia, the Serb jurisdiction with Serbia. NATO troops patrolled the lines of division between them.

The accords also contained, however, provisions for the formation of a single, united Bosnia, which from early 1993 to mid-1995 the Americans had insisted was the only acceptable outcome of the war. Several institutions—a parliament and a central bank, for example—were to include both parts of Bosnia. The American secretary of state, Warren Christopher, repeatedly asserted that the

Dayton accords were *not* a plan for partition. The NATO allies and the warring parties were able to agree on the accords because they incorporated both goals, postponing the question of whether the former Yugoslav republic of Bosnia would ultimately become one or two—or even three—countries.[7]

If the new Western policy of 1995 did not represent a consensus on ends, neither did it reflect an agreement on means. It did not express the conviction that Bosnia was a place important enough to warrant the investment of substantial Western resources. NATO did use force in Bosnia, but only air power. Its members did not send ground troops to fight; even had they been able to agree on what the soldiers were fighting for, such participation in the war would have resulted in casualties that their citizens would not have tolerated. Ground troops were inserted in large numbers only after the shooting had stopped. Even then, the decision to dispatch them was distinctly unpopular among the citizens of the most powerful NATO country, the United States.

For that reason, the Clinton administration promised that the American troops would remain in Bosnia for only one year, hardly enough time to ensure *any* outcome. Moreover, having stopped the fighting, the Western powers declared that the key to Bosnia's future was an expensive effort at economic reconstruction, and then proceeded to squabble over how to pay for it.

The Western initiative in Bosnia in 1995 ultimately stemmed from the conviction that the war was becoming embarrassing, not that it was important. Bosnia was unimportant because the Cold War was over. During the rivalry with the Soviet Union, the NATO countries decided their policies toward Yugoslavia on the basis of their impact on the central conflict in Europe. During the Cold War, therefore, Germany would never have acted independently of its allies and on the basis of domestic political considerations, as it did in forcing international recognition of

Croatian independence.[8] In fact, had the East-West conflict still dominated the foreign policies of the members of the Atlantic Alliance they would likely not have allowed Yugoslavia to disintegrate in the first place.

During the Cold War, the West, principally the United States, provided to the government in Belgrade—which was run by Communists, although of an anti-Soviet stripe—the economic resources to maintain Yugoslavia's national cohesion and the military resources to sustain its independence. The Western goal was to keep Yugoslavia intact in order to prevent it from falling into the Soviet sphere of influence, which Marshal Josip Broz Tito had escaped in the late 1940s. During the Cold War, moreover, the collapse of Yugoslavia would have created a strategic vacuum into which both the Western allies and the Soviet Union and its clients could have been drawn, if only to try to prevent the other side from seizing an advantage there.

During the Cold War, had fighting broken out in Yugoslavia it might have been settled in the same way that fighting in the Balkans was contained prior to World War I. In 1878, the great powers of Europe assembled at Berlin and negotiated a settlement to a conflict triggered by the same kind of nationalist passions that destroyed Yugoslavia in the 1990s, and then imposed that settlement on the warring parties. One of the chief aims of the diplomats at Berlin was to prop up a rickety multinational political structure that governed part of the Balkans. The Ottoman empire was the Yugoslavia of its time, from the ruins of which the union of the south Slavs—Yugoslavia—was partly formed after World War I.

The great powers were determined to put an end to the Balkan conflict in 1878 because they believed that if it went unchecked and the Ottoman empire were allowed to collapse, the scramble for the spoils would draw them into a dangerous conflict with one another. In 1914 that is precisely what happened: A conflict between Austria and

Serbia, the result of the nationalist-inspired assassination by a Serb of the heir to the Habsburg throne, triggered World War I. Restoring peace to the Balkans in 1878 was for the European great powers an exercise in self-defense, as it undoubtedly would have been for their successors, the two nuclear superpowers, during the Cold War. It was a way of forestalling a wider, bloodier conflict in which they would likely have become involved. Pacifying the region therefore commanded the attention and the resources of the governments of the strongest members of the international system.

The necessary condition for the strategic significance of the Balkans in both cases was great-power rivalry, to which this remote, backward, and otherwise insignificant part of Europe was connected through its potential as an arena for that rivalry to be violently played out. Great-power rivalry was, of course, the norm in Europe in the nineteenth, as in previous, centuries. It was the norm, as well, during the Cold War.

With the end of the Cold War, however, this persistent feature of international politics in Europe has—at least temporarily—all but disappeared. With it has disappeared, at least for the moment, the incentive for major powers, including those in NATO, to bury their differences, open their wallets, and above all risk the lives of their troops to stop Balkan peoples from killing one another.[9] Indeed, in the wake of the Cold War the great military powers of Europe seem to be extinct. None of the candidates qualifies: Russia is no longer great, Germany is not military, and the United States, which is both, is not European.

The end, or at least the suspension, of great-power rivalry in the wake of the Cold War has produced a dramatic change in the strategic geography of the international system. During the Cold War the world was, in geopolitical terms, tightly interconnected. Events on the periphery of the international system were believed by the powerful nations at its center to bear directly on their own interests.

The connection between the periphery and the center was expressed in what came to be known as the "domino theory," which held that world politics could be seen as a row of standing dominoes. The toppling of one would set off a chain reaction that would bring down the others.[10] During the Cold War the domino theory had particular resonance. The global aspirations of international communism and the Soviet Union made it easy for the West, particularly the United States, to see connections between those fomenting conflict far away and the forces the West was opposing close to home. It was the Soviet Union that threatened NATO members directly; and it was the Soviet Union that was involved, directly or indirectly, in conflicts in Asia, Africa, and Latin America.[11]

With the end of the Cold War, the disintegration of the Soviet Union, and the disappearance, at least for a time, of great-power rivalry itself, the basis for domino thinking is gone. There is no compelling reason to believe that turbulence on the periphery of the international system will affect its center.[12] For NATO's members, especially the United States, faraway conflicts may be ugly and messy but they are not dangerous. Americans and others recoiled at the images of suffering in Bosnia and elsewhere that television carried around the world. There were limits, however, to what they proved willing to do when the suffering was heart-wrenching but not threatening to them.

This reversal, the abrupt demotion of areas outside Europe to unprecedentedly low status in the West's hierarchy of strategic significance, can be illustrated by a comparison between the Reagan administration's intervention to remove the government of the Caribbean island of Grenada in 1983 and the Clinton administration's ouster of a government it disliked on another Caribbean island, Haiti, eleven years later. By almost any standard Haiti is more important to the United States than Grenada: bigger, more populous, a source of refugees, and a country the United

States occupied between 1915 and 1934. Moreover, Haiti, like the United States, was a destination for Africans brought to the Western Hemisphere as slaves.

There should, therefore, have been wider and deeper political support for intervening in Haiti than in Grenada. To the contrary, the Reagan administration's intervention in Grenada was relatively popular, or at least not decidedly unpopular like the Clinton administration's dispatch of troops to Haiti.

One measure of public support for any military operation is the number of casualties the public is willing to tolerate.[13] Nineteen American troops died in Grenada. The Clinton administration was careful to conduct the invasion and occupation of Haiti in such a way as to minimize the chances that *any* Americans would die in combat there; and none did. The reason for this extraordinary caution was that the public would not tolerate any combat deaths.[14]

The reason for the difference in support for Grenada and Haiti was the presence in the earlier case, and the absence in the later one, of the Cold War. The radical government of Grenada that the Reagan administration unseated was sympathetic to, and received support from, Fidel Castro's Cuba. Cuba was an ally of the Soviet Union, the global adversary of the United States. Removing the Grenadan government could be portrayed as striking a blow at the Soviet Union, albeit at one or two removes. It was a skirmish in a larger ongoing conflict that the United States was waging. It could be seen as an act of self-defense, and thus worth paying a price to achieve.

Haiti, by contrast, had no connection to any larger conflict. Although it violated American standards of democratic governance, the military junta in Port-au-Prince did not threaten the United States even indirectly, except by generating refugees, which the Coast Guard could easily repel.

For the United States, and for Western Europe, Bosnia was more like Haiti than Grenada. Recognizing the domino theory's importance in justifying the use of force on the international periphery, the Clinton administration offered a local version as the rationale for the dispatch of American troops to Bosnia in the latter part of 1995. According to a senior official:

> History and geography have conspired to make Bosnia the most explosive powderkeg on the continent of Europe. Such a conflagration could all too easily spread well beyond the Balkans. Albania could intervene to protect the Albanians who live in the Serbian southern province of Kosovo. Warfare there could unleash a massive flow of refugees into Macedonia . . . potentially drawing in . . . on opposite sides Greece and Turkey . . . If the war in the Balkans is reignited it could spark a wider conflict like those that drew American soldiers into Europe in huge numbers twice in this century.[15]

The administration's policies in Bosnia both before and after the dispatch of troops, however, were at odds with the implications of these words. For thirty months the United States had blocked efforts to end the war, finding the various peace plans that were proposed—the Vance-Owen plan of 1993, the Owen-Stoltenberg plan of 1993, and the Contact Group plan of 1994—insufficiently fair to the Muslim-dominated Sarajevo-based government of Bosnia. From the beginning of 1993 to mid-1995 the American government preferred seeing the war continue to accepting a settlement inconsistent with the principles it then espoused, a position it surely would not have taken had it truly believed that the continuation of the fighting risked triggering World War III. Nor, if officials of the Clinton administration had been genuinely convinced that the resumption of the fighting would "spark a wider conflict" like the two World Wars of the twentieth century, would they have promised that the

American troops enforcing the Dayton accords would be withdrawn from Bosnia after a single year, which risked allowing the fighting to resume.

Where once the core and the periphery had been tightly linked, in the wake of the Cold War they turned out to be strictly separated. A line running east and west came to divide the two, a line running along the southern edge of western and central Europe. Below that line NATO members were extremely reluctant to risk treasure or blood to settle local quarrels.

To summarize: Because the Cold War rivalry was intense, because it involved two opposing coalitions, because each of the two professed a universal ideology, because twentieth-century revolutions in transportation and communication made every part of the world far more accessible to every other part than ever before, almost every corner of every country came to be seen as important, because relevant to the main global rivalry.

Now almost no place is relevant; there is no central rivalry to which it could be relevant. That is the fundamental reason for the failure of NATO to act quickly or decisively in Bosnia. If NATO did not act as an effective police force in Bosnia, it is unlikely to do so elsewhere. The post-Cold War world has turned out to have no shortage of conflicts such as the one in Bosnia, some of them located close to Europe, in the Caucasus, for example, and in Central Asia, in newly independent countries south of Russia that were once republics of the Soviet Union. No Western official, even those most eager to intervene in Bosnia, suggested that NATO launch an out-of-area mission to any of them.

Bosnia was the difficult case. Unlike Georgia, Nagorno-Karabakh, and Tajikistan, it was not easy for NATO members to ignore. The reason, once again, lay in geography. The imaginary post-Cold War line of demarcation between the core and the periphery ran near, or through, Bosnia, which "was, but also was not, a part of Europe."[16]

Bosnia was located astride what was for the West a moral boundary as well. Even in a world without the great-power rivalries that drew the major countries of Europe into the Balkans in the past, the Western powers were not willing to tolerate absolutely anything that transpired on the European periphery. The large-scale brutality and murder in the Balkans caused visceral discomfort, in part because it evoked for many observers memories of the Nazi Holocaust of five decades earlier. It was common to refer to what the Serbs were doing to the Muslims as "genocide."

The result was acute ambivalence, leading to the hesitation, the intra-alliance quarrels, and the gap between words and deeds that marked Western policy. Bosnia was too close, what occurred there was too brutal, to ignore altogether; but the former Yugoslav republic was at the same time too far from Western Europe, with too slight a connection to the security concerns of the West, for the members of NATO to pay a high price to end the fighting there.

Bosnia was the place best suited to a post-Cold War out-of-area NATO mission. Whatever effort the alliance made there, it was likely to do less elsewhere. Thus, despite the Bosnia mission, NATO is not going to transform itself into a global or even a European police force.

There is one basis other than oil on which a place like Bosnia could trigger intervention by the great powers. In the post-Cold War period a tendency has emerged for Russia and the United States to assume a measure of responsibility for keeping order in their neighborhoods. Russia has explicitly adopted a policy to this effect, declaring that it has a special sphere of rights and responsibilities that encompasses the territory of the former Soviet Union.[17]

Washington's intervention in Haiti followed a similar pattern, although with greater hesitation. The United States also intervened to stabilize a neighbor in 1994, when it bailed out Mexico financially after the collapse of the peso.

For Russia, anxious about the threat of instability as well as the spread of Islamic fundamentalism from the

south, and for the United States, worried about the flow of
refugees from south of its borders, intervention after the
Cold War was, as before, an exercise in a kind of self-
defense. Bosnia lies to the south of a large, powerful
European country. But Bosnia's powerful northern neighbor, Germany, has been barred, by tradition and by choice,
from playing a comparable role in the second half of the
twentieth century.[18]

The limits to NATO's activities in Bosnia suggest that
the prospects for out-of-area missions for the Atlantic
Alliance are not promising. This is not welcome news.
Europe and the world would be safer and more peaceful if
those prospects were brighter. The world would benefit
from the existence of a global police force; NATO, as the
most powerful multinational army in the world, is the logical candidate to act in that capacity. Moreover, NATO's
future might rest on a firmer political foundation if its
member states were willing to undertake this role. But they
are not. The alliance will not survive if survival depends on
adopting a new mission to the south; for that reason, among
others, another survival strategy has been proposed: continuing rather than modifying NATO's Cold War mission,
but carrying it out farther to the east.

~3~

EXPANSION

Beyond NATO's eastern border, the eastern border of Germany, lie the four "Visegrad" countries,[1] Poland, Hungary, the Czech Republic, and Slovakia. All seek membership in the Atlantic Alliance. Expanding NATO to include them is, with the assumption of responsibility for out-of-area missions, one of the two major changes that have been proposed for the alliance in the post-Cold War era. Whereas a readiness to respond to out-of-area crises would retain NATO's Cold War membership while giving it a different role, expansion eastward would retain its Cold War purpose while changing its membership.

The two versions of NATO have important similarities. They share the same purposes: to address a potential post-Cold War problem in Europe and to provide a rationale for the continuation of NATO. The alliance has made a commitment to each: in practice, to an out-of-area mission through the operation in Bosnia; in principle, to expansion. In January 1994, President Bill Clinton declared that the question of extending membership eastward was "no longer whether . . . but when and how. . . ."[2]

Both are latter-day versions of initiatives advanced after the earlier great European conflicts of modern times: Out-of-area missions are the post-Cold War equivalent of the suggestion that the victorious powers police the continent. Underlying the idea of NATO expansion is the perennial postwar impulse to contain the defeated power to prevent it from making another bid for mastery of Europe.

Each version has a major drawback, however: Out-of-area missions are desirable but not feasible—Western publics will not provide the political support that military operations of this kind require. NATO expansion is feasible but not desirable. Its benefits are more modest than its advocates claim, and its disadvantages more severe, for the three groups of countries that expansion would affect: NATO's existing members, the prospective Central European members, and Russia.

Like the adoption of an out-of-area role, extending NATO eastward is supposed to give the alliance a purpose that can justify its continued existence in the eyes of the publics of its member countries, particularly the United States. President Clinton reportedly made this case to Russian president Boris Yeltsin, arguing that Russia had an interest in maintaining an American role in Europe and that expanding NATO was the best way to assure this.[3]

Expanding NATO, however, would be costly, if not in troops then at least in military assistance to new members. The additional expense would not be welcome in the United States at a time when reducing expenditures for domestic programs in an effort to lower the American government's budget deficit has become a priority of both the Congress and the president. Spending more on NATO would run counter to one of the strongest political currents of the post-Cold War era in the West: reducing defense budgets. Two months after voting for NATO expansion, in fact, the American Congress voted against increasing funds for upgrading NATO equipment and facilities.[4]

Nor would the American public be eager to bear what might be the greater military risks that eastward expansion would bring. The alliance's new members would presumably receive the same guarantee that the United States gave to the original members: a promise to defend them in case of attack with whatever military means are necessary, including nuclear weapons. In the NATO of the Cold War, a nuclear conflict in Europe had the potential to spread across the Atlantic; this meant that, in pledging to resist a Soviet assault on Bonn or West Berlin, the United States was accepting the risk of a retaliatory Soviet attack on New York.

In an expanded NATO, the United States would have to make the same promise and run the same risks for Bratislava, the capital of Slovakia, as it did for Cold War Bonn. A public unwilling to risk the lives of American servicemen to protect the Bosnian capital of Sarajevo would be even less likely to authorize risking the annihilation of American cities and the deaths of millions of American civilians to protect a less familiar Central European capital. A NATO commitment to defend Bratislava might prove easy to give because the Slovak capital appears to be in no danger. But this very lack of danger raises the question of why such a commitment should be given at all.[5]

Germany shares with the United States the belief that the perpetuation of NATO is necessary for the sake of tasks that remain important but may no longer command support, not the least of which is reassuring Germany about Russia while at the same time reassuring Russia and the rest of Europe about Germany.[6] The Germans have an additional reason for favoring the expansion of the Atlantic Alliance to the east. After World War II, Germany was reintegrated into Western Europe through membership in international organizations—the European Common Market and NATO. This enabled Germany to establish good relations with countries that had recently been its enemies and had suffered mightily at German hands; it put Germany and its neighbors on an equal footing and offered a ready-made framework for containing its power, thus alleviating its neighbors' anxieties.

Of all its neighbors, indeed of all the countries of Europe, none suffered more at German hands during World War II than Poland. Even five decades later, with Germany significantly different in every important way from the Third Reich, Polish memories and the fears they evoked were not entirely extinguished. Thus Poles and Germans want Poland in NATO for the same reason that the French and the Germans want Germany in NATO: to put their bilateral relationship in a multilateral context in order to ease the lingering concerns that the horrible events of the past, and the disparities in wealth and power of the present, could raise.

NATO membership for Poland is not, however, a prerequisite for good Polish-German relations. Polish fears have a powerful basis in the past but not in the present. Post-Cold War Germany is not only democratic and peaceful but has also clearly affirmed, as the border between the two countries, the Oder-Neisse line, which was drawn by Stalin to incorporate historically German territories into Poland. Since German unification there has been no hint of German irredentism or even unfriendliness toward Poland. In addition, a lively trade between the two countries has been established.

The perpetuation of NATO's Cold War structure would keep Germany firmly anchored in a multilateral security organization even without Polish membership. Nor have Poland or the other three Visegrad countries been excluded from full membership in the European Union, a goal both they and the EU members have endorsed. Thus NATO membership for the Visegrad Four is not indispensable for putting their relations with Germany on a multilateral basis, nor for obtaining one of the chief security advantages—reassurance—of doing so.

Moreover, if some Germans favored NATO expansion, many other Europeans were skeptical, dubious, or opposed.

Although European governments did not take public exception to President Clinton's call for expansion, privately they sought to slow or halt the process. Even if the American public were to unite in support of NATO, therefore, the issue had the potential to divide the alliance's member governments.[7]

The Germans had another reason for favoring Polish membership in NATO: an understandable desire not to continue to be the alliance's easternmost outpost. For four decades Germany had been a "front-line state," with the dividing line between east and west in Europe running through its territory. The Germans did not want, nor did they necessarily anticipate, a post-Cold War line of division on the continent, but if there were to be one, they preferred that it be drawn as far east as possible—for example, along the eastern border of Poland rather than that of Germany.

The case for NATO expansion involves, as well, the benefits it would purportedly bring to the new members themselves. Specifically, its advocates argued that NATO membership would promote desirable political developments and thwart poisonous political trends in formerly Communist Europe.

NATO membership for the Visegrad Four, its proponents claimed, would support democracy and free markets in these countries. With the overthrow of communism they installed democratic governments, which, however, were fragile, according to this argument. NATO membership would consolidate democracy in part of post-Communist Europe as it did in Germany in the 1950s and in Spain, Portugal, and Greece in the 1970s and 1980s.

The analogy is misleading. The United States occupied Germany after World War II; and Portugal and Greece were NATO members even while they were under authoritarian rule. Moreover, seven years after the overthrow of communism, democracy did not appear visibly threatened in Poland, Hungary, or the Czech Republic; nor was their citizens' determination to be part of Western Europe faltering. The post-Communist parties that won control of the governments of Hungary in 1994 and Poland in 1995 turned out to be as committed as were their anti-Communist predecessors to both goals.

The post-Communist dangers the countries of Central Europe faced—the obstacles to the construction of stable Western political and economic institutions—were poverty, unemployment, ethnic strife, and the weight of the Communist past with its legacy of individual suspicion, passivity, and authoritarian rule. To the extent that democracy and free markets could be strengthened by membership in a Western organization, the appropriate one was not NATO but the European Union.

For this there is an important precedent. The transfusion of dollars through the Marshall Plan after World War II was crucial for Western European countries, some with little experience of democratic governance, all suffering from economic dislocation, and many plagued by forces of political extremism prepared to capitalize on both. Economic stability followed by prosperity nurtured democracy in Western Europe after 1945. Economic stability and prosperity are important for sustaining democracy in Central and Eastern Europe after the Cold War, but membership in NATO will not provide them. Economic access to Western Europe, including, ultimately, membership in the European Union, is far more relevant.*

*The Visegrad Four did seek EU membership but came to see NATO as the organization they could join more quickly. For this there were some good reasons: EU membership requires economic harmony with the West in ways that were difficult for the countries of Central and Eastern Europe to achieve in the short term. But among the obstacles to the rapid entry of Central Europe into the EU was also an inward-looking, protectionist bias in Western Europe. In the post-Cold War era it seemed politically easier for Western governments to agree to risk nuclear annihilation in order to protect Hungary's borders, for example, than to allow their own citizens to buy Hungarian tomatoes.

To the extent, moreover, that NATO membership *is* relevant to assisting in the development of stable democratic politics, it was being contemplated for the wrong countries. The most appropriate candidates were not the Visegrad Four but rather Russia and Ukraine, where five years after the collapse of the Soviet Union democracy was shakier and the stakes for the West were higher because of the importance of the countries themselves. From the Western perspective, democracy in Slovakia was undoubtedly desirable; but democracy in Russia was a strategic asset of far greater value, worth a very great deal to achieve.[8]

The poisonous trend in Central and Eastern Europe that NATO membership is supposed to thwart is ethnic conflict similar to that in Bosnia. In defense of expansion, American officials invoked the vision of "a NATO which is reaching out to the east, which is trying to prevent . . . repetition of what has happened in the former Yugoslavia."[9] It was this hoped-for effect of including Central Europe in the alliance to which Volker Ruehe referred when he asserted, "Either we will export stability or we will end up importing instability."[10] NATO expansion according to this view is designed to respond to what Secretary of State Warren Christopher described as the post-Cold War threat to Western interests: "not invasion from the East but instability in the West."[11]

As with its putative role as a catalyst for democracy, however, as an antidote to ugly civil strife NATO membership was being offered to the wrong countries. Post-Communist Poland, Hungary, the Czech Republic, and Slovakia were, especially by the standards of Central and Eastern Europe, decidedly homogeneous in ethnic terms, especially after the 1990 "velvet divorce" between the Czechs and Slovaks.[12] Moreover, given the widespread Western aversion to becoming involved in Bosnia itself, it was unclear why the citizens of NATO's member countries would leap at the chance to participate in other, similar conflicts. Furthermore, on the question of calming ethnic strife

the argument in favor of NATO expansion contained a contradiction. One of the conditions for membership announced
by the alliance was freedom from precisely such conflicts.
Thus NATO membership seemed to be available for the
purpose of preventing ethnic conflict only to countries that
did not have any.

Nor was it clear how NATO membership, by itself,
would stifle the kind of conflict over the control of territory
and political power that erupted in the former Yugoslavia.
Membership in NATO had not prevented Turkey from
using force against the Greek Cypriots in 1974, although it
may have limited the conflict between Turkey and Greece
itself.

There was, in fact, an air of evasion about the case for
NATO expansion as presented by its member governments,
especially the government of the United States. Their stated
reasons rang hollow because these were not the real reasons,
or at least not the only ones. Some of the American impetus
for including the Visegrad Four in the Atlantic Alliance
stemmed from domestic politics. The president sought to
enhance his standing among voters with family ties to those
countries, who happened to be clustered in states crucial to
his chances for reelection in 1996.[13] This is a form of interest
group politics familiar in American public life, which has,
however, seldom determined major strategic initiatives such
as the construction or major extension of the nation's principal overseas military and political commitment.

It would have been impolitic for the Clinton administration to say that it wanted to expand NATO in order to
win votes at home. Nor could it, for other reasons, advance
the one genuinely strategic rationale for bringing Central
and Eastern Europe into the alliance, a rationale embraced
by both Western supporters of the idea and the prospective
new members themselves. This was an updated, modified
version of the alliance's traditional purpose. NATO had
been founded during the Cold War to contain the Soviet

Union. It should be expanded in the post-Cold War era, according to this view, to contain the Soviet Union's principal successor state: Russia.

While the first option for post-Cold War NATO, the maintenance of the status quo, is a cure for uncertainty, and the second, the adoption of out-of-area missions, is a response to instability, the third—expansion to the east—is a hedge against outright aggression. The first is directed at Germany, the second at Bosnia, the third at Russia. A larger Western coalition, reaching farther to the east than the original NATO, is thought by some advocates of NATO expansion to be necessary for containing a smaller, less powerful, but still potentially dangerous Russia.

It is this reason for NATO expansion that hearkens back to an impulse palpable in the wake of the other great European conflicts of modern times: the impulse to design a European order in which the power just defeated at great cost would be prevented from attempting another round of conquest or intimidation. After the Napoleonic Wars and World War I, the victors carved new states out of the territory of the losers, to serve as buffers between France and then Germany on the one hand and the rest of Europe on the other. After World War II, the defeated power was occupied, and most of the lesser states were incorporated into the military and political coalitions of one or the other of the two extra-European nuclear superpowers. NATO expansion would combine the two approaches. The newly liberated countries of Central and Eastern Europe would be absorbed into the Western coalition, as a way of "consolidating the gains of the Cold War."[14]

This third and most coherent rationale for NATO expansion was based on the assumption that Russia would, in all likelihood, resume an aggressive, imperial foreign policy. The Clinton administration could not say this publicly because it had made the promotion of democracy and free markets in Russia, for the sake of fostering peaceful Russian relations with its neighbors, a cornerstone of its foreign policy. But others could and did say it.

> Russia is already getting back on its feet geopolitically, even before it gets back on its feet economically. The only potential great-power security problem in Central Europe is the lengthening shadow of Russian strength, and NATO still has the job of counterbalancing it. Russia is a force of nature; all this is inevitable.[15]

This view of Russia and Europe is not groundless. The history of the Russian and then the Soviet state for four centuries is one of expansion in all directions from its Muscovite core. While the past is not an infallible guide to the future, it is surely relevant. The prospective Central European members of NATO are only too acutely aware of that history. Their concern that history would repeat itself prompted them to seek protection against that eventuality in the form of NATO membership.

Historically the countries between Russia and Germany were pawns in the chess game of great-power politics in Europe. As such, they were often sacrificed by one side or the other. Sovereign independence was an all too brief experience. Usually the Central Europeans were part of a larger entity—an empire or a sphere of influence dominated by more powerful nations or dynasties. If that pattern was to continue in the post-Cold War era, the Central Europeans at least wished to be able to choose the larger community to which they would belong. This was the option that had been denied them, in effect at gunpoint, after World War II. Occupied by the Red Army, they became, unwillingly but inevitably, given the distribution of military power in Europe, Communist satellites of the Soviet Union.

Even if Russia is destined to resume an imperial foreign policy, however, the proposed pattern of NATO expansion is flawed. As is the case if the alliance is presumed to be a school for democracy, expanding its membership to Central Europe does not take it far enough east. The countries most vulnerable to an aggressive Russia are the now-independent former Soviet republics that are Russia's western neighbors: the three Baltic states—Estonia, Latvia, and Lithuania—as well as Ukraine and Belarus. Unlike them, three of the Visegrad countries have no common border with Russia.* Plans for an expanded NATO did not, however, include the former Soviet republics, at least initially.[16]

They would be left without a formal association with the West but facing a Russia that the advocates of NATO expansion presumed would be pursuing a predatory foreign policy. They would find themselves on the exposed side of a new line of division in Europe.[17] As with the promotion of democracy and ethnic harmony, therefore, so with the plans for expanding NATO in order to enhance European security: Those that needed it would not get it; those that got it would not need it.

During the Cold War, it was sometimes charged that, at their meeting with Stalin at Yalta on the Black Sea in February 1945 to plan the postwar world, the leaders of the Western powers, Roosevelt and Churchill, had "sold out" the countries of Central and Eastern Europe. The site of that meeting became an international code word for betrayal, for giving Stalin tacit permission to impose brutal, illegitimate Communist regimes on the people of the region.[18]

---

*Poland is an exception. Kaliningrad, formerly German Königsberg, on the Baltic remains Russian territory, although separated from the Russian mainland by Lithuania. It has a heavy concentration of military forces. Moreover, the future as an independent state of Belarus, which has a 360-mile border with Poland, is uncertain. The president elected in 1994, Alexander Lukashenko, advocated rejoining Russia, and in April 1996, Russia and Belarus signed an accord committing them to union with each other.

The charge is without merit. The Central Europeans did find themselves in the wrong camp, an experience that, in the wake of the Cold War, they were understandably determined not to repeat. But this was not the fault of the West. However naive or maladroit Churchill and Roosevelt's dealings with Stalin may have been, the fate of the countries between Germany and the Soviet Union was determined by the course of the war against Hitler. The Soviets, advancing from the east, and the Americans and British, attacking from the west, exercised control over the territories they occupied during the course of the war. Stalin could not have been evicted from the territory the Red Army had conquered except by force; and there was never any serious sentiment in the West for an anti-Soviet campaign to liberate Eastern Europe, even at a time when the United States enjoyed a monopoly of atomic weapons.

What the West was wrongly accused of doing to Central Europe in the wake of World War II, however, it would risk doing to Ukraine and the Baltic states in the wake of the Cold War by expanding NATO as planned, thus stranding these former Soviet republics outside the Western alliance system at the mercy of a rapacious Russia. To be sure, NATO's inclusion of the Visegrad Four would not guarantee that Ukraine and the Baltic states would suffer such a fate; but the strategically coherent case for extending the alliance to Central Europe rests on a view of Russia that suggests that they would. And if they did, what was true of the Central European countries in the late 1940s could not be said of the fate of the western former Soviet republics: that it was unavoidable.

What happens to the countries between Russia and Germany depends heavily on the policies of Russia and Germany themselves. The future of Germany, a firmly democratic country, is predictable. The future of Russia, by contrast, is uncertain.[19] Russia is not destined to take any particular course. Moscow may resume the imperial policies that were so prominent and consistent a part of Russian history; but it may not. Beginning in 1989 and continuing for four years thereafter, through the collapse of the Soviet Union and the emergence of a new, smaller, more ethnically homogeneous Russia, the thrust of Russian foreign policy was the opposite of imperial. Soviet forces withdrew from the countries that had belonged to the Warsaw Treaty Organization. After the collapse of the Soviet Union itself, Russian forces quit the Baltic states. Russia accepted the formation of an independent Ukrainian army. Perhaps, under the eyes of eternity, the retreat will prove to have been merely temporary; but there is nothing foreordained about this. Russia, like other organized political communities, is capable of sharp, sustained changes of direction. It is not programmed to follow any one particular political course. It is subject to influence, including the influence of other countries.

That is to say, the West can affect the course of Russian foreign policy. It was the central purpose of Western foreign policy during the Cold War to affect the course of Soviet foreign policy; but in the wake of the Cold War the range of possibilities is wider. Then, the malevolent intentions of the Soviet leadership were clear, fixed, and unshakable. The task of the West was to muster countervailing power sufficient to keep Moscow from attempting to act on those intentions.

In the wake of the Cold War, it is the intentions themselves—more broadly, Russians' own definition of what their role in the world and their relations with their neighbors ought to be—that are fluid. The test of Western policy is how it affects those intentions.

If the extension of membership in the Atlantic Alliance to the countries of Central Europe were likely to make Russia *less* likely to pursue the kinds of policies its imperial and Communist predecessors followed, this would count strongly in favor of expansion. And it is conceivable that NATO expansion could close off, in Russian eyes, the option of reconstituting the Soviet empire, thus discrediting Russian advocates of neo-imperialism.[20] It is conceivable that membership for the Visegrad Four in the Atlantic Alliance would improve Russian behavior abroad.

This argument is not, however, convincing to those who know Russia best: Russians themselves. In particular, Russian democrats have declared themselves adamantly opposed to NATO expansion, seeing it as a blow to their cause, perhaps even a crippling handicap in the struggle among Russians over the country's future. The outcome of that struggle was less certain, because the forces of democracy and free markets were weaker, in Russia than in Central and Eastern Europe, where there was a consensus on the need to be like, and to belong to, the West.

While Russian democrats were committed to good relations with the West, and to eventual integration into Europe and the international community, the extreme nationalists and hardline Communists among their political opponents were not. As one group of liberal Russian foreign policy experts put it: "In Russia . . . various forces seek to provoke a crisis in our relations with the outside world, so that the country would once again find herself in a malign encirclement, haunted by the 'complex of besieged': for some of them, this is the only available way to power, for others, this is the means to strengthen their hold on power with an 'iron hand.'"[21] NATO expansion, Russian democrats asserted, would be taken as a Western vote of no confidence in their objectives, a sign that the West did not believe that a peaceful, democratic Russia was possible but rather thought that post-Communist Russia would resume the foreign policy of imperial Russia and the Soviet Union, as an aggressive power to be isolated and contained. According to these experts, " . . . it is from this point of view, which is political and psychological, that NATO enlargement contradicts Russia's national interests. The danger lies in the emergence of the feeling of military and political isolation of Russia, in the revival of anti-Western and militaristic trends in the public."[22]

Russian hypernationalists and unreconstructed Communists favored the revival of such trends. It was with these most dangerous elements of Russian politics that the proponents of NATO expansion were, in the eyes of Russian democrats, unintentionally making common cause. NATO expansion was, in effect, a prophecy about the Russian future that Russian democrats feared would become self-fulfilling.

The course of Russian politics and the character of the Russian political system will be more heavily influenced by internal than international developments, and international influences that do affect it will not come exclusively from the West.[23] But the policies of other countries, especially Western countries, will surely affect the course of Russian foreign policy, and NATO expansion is not likely to affect Russian foreign policy in a way that would contribute to stability and harmony in Europe.

The official Russian response to the prospect of including Central Europe in the Atlantic Alliance was strongly negative and occasionally overheated. At the outset of 1995 Boris Yeltsin complained that the prospect of NATO expansion was "sowing the seeds of mistrust" and that Europe was "in danger of plunging into a Cold Peace."[24] Later the same year he said that "those who insist on an expansion of NATO are making a major political mistake. The flame of war could burst out across the whole of Europe."[25] War would almost certainly not be the immediate consequence of the inclusion of some or all of the Visegrad countries in NATO. The expansion of the alliance would be taken as an offense but not as an act of war by Russia, which is in any case too weak to mount a serious campaign of military opposition. In the short term, Russia would have no choice but to accept NATO expansion, albeit grudgingly.[26]

Russia would, however, have various options for responding in the short term that, if acted upon, would not be welcome in the West. Moscow could try to make the Confederation of Independent States (CIS), the loose association of most of the former Soviet republics, a real military organization and the eastern pillar of a new, bipolar structure of power in Europe. This could entail putting pressure on Ukraine, which has remained outside the CIS, to join it. Russia could also withhold cooperation with the West on the control of nuclear material, including nuclear weapons, on the territory of the former Soviet Union. It could delay ratification of, or repudiate altogether, arms limitation treaties that it has signed. It could seek to increase the strength of the military forces stationed on its western borders, put those and other forces on a higher state of alert, or place greater emphasis in defense planning on nuclear weapons.

The greatest danger of NATO expansion, however, is its possible effect on Russian foreign policy over the long term. It has the potential to turn the country against the entire post-Cold War settlement in Europe, a settlement that is extraordinarily favorable to the West. By the terms of that settlement the Soviet Union, and then Russia, gave up the positions and the ambitions over which the Cold War was waged, but without the carnage and destruction of an actual war. The Soviet empire was dismantled, Russian power retreated and disintegrated, the countries old and new between Berlin and Vladivostok overthrew Communist regimes and installed democratic or at least less repressive governments, and Russia itself became smaller—with its borders located farther to the north and east—than at any time in the last three centuries.

Yet this was not a dictated peace. Russia accepted all these changes voluntarily. The Soviet and then the Russian government took part and acquiesced in all the events that produced the settlement, which has, therefore, a measure of legitimacy in Russian eyes. This legitimacy is a priceless asset for the West.

But Russians of all political persuasions have made it clear that they will not accept the eastward extension of NATO voluntarily. NATO expansion therefore runs the risk of creating a consensus within Russia that not only this particular measure but also the entire post-Cold War settlement is arbitrary, unfair, and anti-Russian. Such a development could make the overturning of the settlement a central aim of future Russian foreign policy, no matter who is responsible for conducting it.[27]

Moreover, if the Russian people were to turn against the international consequences of the collapse of the Soviet Union, that could discredit the regime—indeed the type of regime—that had presided over the culmination of that collapse and accepted its consequences. This was what happened in Germany after World War I.[28]

After World War I, as after the Cold War, the defeated power lost territory, on which were established new countries that formed a *cordon sanitaire*, a security belt, around the loser. But it was not simply the creation of the successor states to the Habsburg empire—the countries of Central Europe that, seventy-five years later, aspired to join NATO—that turned the Germans against the post-World War I settlement. It was also the unexpected assignment to Germany of the responsibility for starting the war, embodied in Clause 231 of the Versailles Treaty, on the basis of which the allied powers demanded reparations from the Germans, that poisoned German attitudes to the peace settlement.[29] Resentment of Versailles never died in Germany, and when Hitler came to power with the aid of the Great Depression, his determined and successful policy of overturning the treaty was wildly popular. It was that policy, of course, that culminated in World War II.

NATO expansion is, in the eyes of Russians in the 1990s, what the war guilt clause was for Germans in the 1930s: It reneges on the terms on which they believe the conflict with the West ended. It is a betrayal of the understanding they thought they had with their former enemies. Just as the Germans believed that they would participate, after World War I, in what Woodrow Wilson had promised, a "peace without victors," so the Russians believed that, with the end of the Cold War, they would become the partners of the West. In the wake of that conflict the West's goal for Russia, at least rhetorically, continued to be integration and assimilation. On May 10, 1995, in Moscow, Presidents Clinton and Yeltsin issued a joint statement endorsing "the integration of all of Europe into a series of mutually supporting institutions and relations which ensure . . . [no] division or confrontation."[30] NATO expansion, however, was consistent with the opposite policy: the isolation and exclusion of Russia on the assumption that it could not be assimilated into the West and the international community.

Thus, in conjunction with the rise of extremist forces in domestic Russian politics, over the long term NATO expansion could produce the worst nightmare of the post-Cold War era: Weimar Russia.

To summarize: NATO expansion is likely to be ineffective as a vehicle either for sustaining popular enthusiasm for the continuation of NATO or for consolidating democracy in the Central European countries that have been implicitly promised membership. To these worthy goals NATO membership is largely irrelevant. Alliance expansion eastward is all too relevant, however, to another equally worthy and, from the point of view of Western interests, more important goal: preventing the rise of a Russian threat to Russia's immediate neighbors and to the rest of Europe. For this goal, NATO expansion is likely to prove counterproductive, helping to create the threat it is intended to resist.

NATO expansion would also be a measure of dubious international legality. It would violate at least the spirit of German unification, which implied a bargain between East and West: The Soviet Union had allowed a united Germany to be part of NATO in order to assure its firm anchoring in the West. The West agreed in turn not to bring NATO's military might nearer the Soviet borders, an agreement that included the territory of the former East Germany. Between the opening of the Berlin Wall in 1989 and the formal union of Communist East Germany with the German Federal Republic in 1990, the West offered assurances to Moscow that, although not of the binding character of formal treaties, are at least inconsistent with the inclusion of countries to the east of Germany as full-fledged members of NATO. At the "Open Skies" conference in Ottawa on February 12, 1990, when the Soviet Union agreed to the "two-plus-four" format for settling the future of Germany, which involved the two German states and the four countries with occupation rights in Germany stemming from World War II, "the Western Foreign Ministers . . . agreed not to extend NATO to the east and to let the Soviets know that the Western Alliance would not accept the former Warsaw Pact states as members in NATO."[31]

Central European membership in the Atlantic Alliance would also violate the spirit if not the letter of the treaty on Conventional Forces in Europe (CFE), which allocated quotas of designated armaments to different countries under a particular set of political circumstances: In 1990, when it was signed, the prospective new members of NATO were no longer aligned with the Soviet Union but were not part of a Western military organization either. The CFE treaty was modified in 1992 to take into account the dissolution of the Soviet Union, the total armaments for which were apportioned among its western successor states. Because none of the countries between Russia and Germany was part of any military bloc when the totals were allocated, all kept the weapons they had originally been assigned. NATO expansion would undercut the political assumption that undergirded these assignments.

The CFE treaty is relevant to a final consideration that bears on NATO expansion. Beyond the claims that this will promote particular internal practices or institutions, or that it is necessary to contain Russia, stands a more general argument: *Some* security structure is needed between Russia and Germany, and in the wake of the Cold War there is none. The extension of NATO eastward is thus necessary to fill what the end of the East-West rivalry has created: a vacuum.[32] The term implies at worst chaos, at best an empty space that ultimately will be occupied by something and therefore should be occupied by something benign—the Atlantic Alliance. NATO expansion thus purports to answer the need for a new security architecture in Europe.

In fact, there is no vacuum. There is, instead, a new, different, and supremely valuable security order in place, not simply between Germany and Russia but throughout Europe, from the Atlantic to the Urals. Central to this new security order are the CFE treaty and other arms control accords that were negotiated in the last years of the Cold War and the early years of the post-Cold War era. The existence of this new security order is the basis for the most telling arguments against NATO expansion: It is unnecessary, because the solution to the problem to which expansion is intended to respond is already in place; and it is unwise, because NATO expansion could overturn the new order that forms the basis for this solution.

This is a large claim. To support it, to understand why and how a new, different, and better security order is already in place, requires a detour from the issues of the moment to a review of the fundamental elements of security and the character of the international system.

The shift of narrative gears in the next chapter, to a more abstract level of analysis, has two purposes. First, the new security order is radical in that it goes to the root of the general problem of international security. To appreciate it requires revisiting that problem's basic features. Second, while the separate elements of the new security order are familiar, the way in which, collectively, they form something without precedent in European history is not. The post-Cold War security order in Europe is new and different precisely by virtue of the relationship of its constituent parts to one another, the way that the combination of them transcends older, more familiar patterns of international relations.

The new order may be compared to a marching band performing during the halftime of a college football game. Close up it appears to be lines and clusters of students in colorful uniforms playing musical instruments. At a distance, high above the field, the band members can be seen to form distinct shapes or words, often the name of their school. The larger pattern is discernible only from a distance. The purpose of the next chapter is to provide such a perspective—an aerial view of the general problem of international security, the better to see what has been created on the ground in post-Cold War Europe.

~Part II~

COMMON SECURITY

~4~

THE FOUNDATIONS OF
INTERNATIONAL SECURITY

International conflict has two types of causes. The more
familiar kind consists of the large category of goals, aspirations, and ideologies over which sovereign states have
traditionally gone to war. They are the subject of political
history as it has always been written.

There is, however, a second cause of organized conflict:
the underlying structure of the system of sovereign states.
That structure is anarchic. The international system lacks a
government to guide and regulate the conduct of its members and to punish misconduct. Each state is at risk of attack
from others in the sense that there is no supreme authority
to prevent this. The international order is thus a system in
which independent countries must be prepared at all times
to defend themselves against others.

For students of international politics, war is the consequence of the combination of the "state-level" causes that

history has always provided and this second, pervasive, continuous "system-level" cause, the international anarchy that dates in the West at least from the time of the ancient Greeks. Sovereign states fight for the motives that make up international history; but they are free to fight because of anarchy, because there is nothing to stop them.

The fact of the underlying anarchy has an independent effect on the foreign policies of sovereign states, although it is not easy to detect and has seldom been central to the decision-making process in international relations. State-level causes of war are offensive, based on what sovereign states want. System-level causes are defensive, based on what states fear. Even in the absence of state-level causes of conflict, the world would be a potentially dangerous and therefore perpetually insecure place because the defensive causes of conflict would continue to operate.

As Thucydides put it, "among neighbors antagonism is ever a condition of independence."[1] Others, after all, might attack; anarchy means that there is nothing to stop them. To be safe within the international system has always meant being prepared. Being unprepared may invite attack; overt military preparations, by contrast, may discourage aggression.

Such measures, however, can also have the opposite effect. Preparations for defense may appear to benignly inclined neighbors as evidence of hostile intent. Although not intended to be hostile, military preparedness can trigger actions by neighbors that similarly have defensive motives but nonetheless appear aggressive.

The fact that either of two opposite reactions to the same policy is possible is, in the parlance of students of international relations, the security dilemma. It arises from the fact that threats and preparations to meet them are interrelated in unpredictable ways.[2] Because the effect on others of one's own policies is unpredictable, it seems better to err on the side of caution. Preparations to defend oneself may discourage attack.

Even if they have the unintended and indeed unwanted effect of provoking aggressive policies where none previously existed, they also give the state carrying them out the means to cope with such aggression.

Because it will always seem better to be safe than sorry, and being safe means being armed, the anarchic structure of the international system would make the world an armed camp even in the absence of the familiar state-level reasons for conflict. The logical tendency for sovereign states to cope with the security dilemma in this way is the premise of the "realist" interpretation of international politics, according to which the principle of "better safe than sorry," implemented by the acquisition of arms, gets adopted universally and becomes a self-fulfilling prophecy: Each sovereign state acts as if others might be aggressive, which creates a world of anxious, conflict-ready preparedness all apart from any particular goals or aspirations harbored by any of them. For this reason, international relations have exhibited certain fundamental features continuously for 2,500 years of recorded history in the West.*

In theory, wars can be conflicts of pure anarchy, arising not from specific national political goals but rather out of the poisonous interaction of misunderstanding and mistrust

---

*See John J. Mearsheimer, "The False Promise of International Institutions," *International Security*, Winter 1994–95, p. 7. The realist view of international politics is a variant of a more general problem to which political scientists and economists have devoted considerable attention, the problem of "cooperation under anarchy." It is also called the "free rider" or "public goods" problem and is captured by the situation known as "the Prisoner's Dilemma." In all these variants, a desirable outcome that requires all members of a group to follow a particular policy—known generically as "cooperation"—is difficult to attain because no individual member has an incentive to act in a cooperative way. To the contrary, it is rational for each to behave in "uncooperative" fashion. Thus uncooperative action, which is rational for each, produces an outcome that is worse for all than what universal cooperation would have yielded. *Ibid.*, p. 17.

that the system's underlying anarchy makes possible. In such a case the warring parties are Othellos, driven to tragically unnecessary acts by unfounded suspicions of others. Unlike for Othello, these suspicions are rooted not in human nature but in the underlying anarchy of the international system.[3]

Whether any actual conflict can be said to have been purely the product of anarchy-inspired mistrust is debatable. Perhaps the best-known candidate for the distinction is the Peloponnesian War between Athens and Sparta in fifth-century-B.C. Greece according to the interpretation of the historian Thucydides, or rather according to one often-cited sentence in Thucydides' account: "What made war inevitable was the growth of Athenian power and the fear which this caused in Sparta."[4]

Contemporary conflicts have sometimes been imputed to fears that stem ultimately from anarchy. The origins of the Soviet-American rivalry after World War II have been said to lie in each side's misunderstanding of, and overreaction to, the other's concerns about its own security. Similarly, the Sino-American conflict in Korea in 1950, according to some scholars, stemmed from the Communist government in Beijing's mistaken conviction that the United States was seeking to reverse the Communist triumph of the previous year in the Chinese civil war.[5]

While misunderstanding may have aggravated these conflicts, however, it did not create them out of thin air. In neither case were state-level causes of conflict absent. To the contrary, the United States and the Soviet Union were profoundly at odds over how the countries of Europe should be governed as well as over the distribution of power and influence on the European continent. Similarly, the democratic United States and Communist China had sharp disagreements over a wide range of issues, including how Korea should be governed.

Historically, in fact, it is difficult to find conflicts arising solely out of pure anarchy, wars in which state-level causes played no role at all. State-level causes—what historians identify as the causes of war—have always been present. But anarchy, too, has always been present. To explain a particular war as the result of anarchy is like imputing a plane crash to gravity. It is true at some level, but also trivial or at least unhelpful because, while other causes of crashes, having to do with equipment malfunction and pilot error, can be fixed, gravity cannot be repealed.

The anarchy of international politics is, in this sense, different from gravity. It is not a force of nature. It is part of how human beings have chosen to organize themselves politically. Unlike gravity it can, in theory, be abolished or modified. If the opposite principle, hierarchy, were substituted for anarchy, war could be prevented. Hierarchy—government—would do for the society of sovereign states, where it does not exist, what it does for societies of individuals: provide the basis for law and order.

World government has had its advocates, especially in the wake of the great wars of the twentieth century, conflicts in which the costs of anarchy have been painfully high. But the advocates have never come close to achieving what they have proposed. World government has been more a utopian fantasy than a practical program. It belongs to the history of ideas about international politics but not to the history of international politics itself, despite the establishment, in the twentieth century, of two international organizations with universal membership and institutions resembling those of a government. Neither the League of Nations nor the United Nations, however, ever had, or was intended to have, the powers of a government. Neither ever had the most important attribute of a government, a legal monopoly of force. Even in the wake of the two bloodiest conflicts of the twentieth century, sovereign states have not been willing to surrender their independence to a global Leviathan. The appeal of sovereignty has outweighed its dangers. In fact, with the disintegration of the multinational empires that had controlled most of the planet in previous centuries and the emergence from their ruins of many independent countries, the twentieth century has seen the proliferation not the sublimation of sovereignty. Nor does the end of the Cold War seem likely to reverse this trend. It brought about the collapse of two Communist empires out of which came, in the case of the Soviet Union, eighteen new sovereign states, and in the Yugoslav case, five.

Sovereignty has persisted because its dangers are limited, not fatal. War is awful, especially in the twentieth century, but not awful beyond the capacity of citizens to bear it. Nor is it constant. Typically, war only occasionally interrupts longer periods of wary armed peace. It is compatible with the survival of most sovereign states and with a normal life for most of their inhabitants most of the time.

Thus world government has not been established because war is bearable; war is bearable because it is not constant; and war is not constant because it can be, and has been, prevented by a method other than world government. It is known as the balance of power. The term refers to a roughly even distribution of military might between and among the strongest members of the international system.

From the "realist" perspective, a stable balance of power is the best of all possible worlds, the only basis for peace that is both dependable and achievable. A stable balance of power is in effect when sovereign states are independent, wary, and armed, but when the distribution of military power among them is such that none is tempted to attack any other because none believes it can prevail, at least not at an acceptable cost.

The peace, or at least the absence of direct combat, between the United States and the Soviet Union during the Cold War was sustained, in the face of powerful state-level reasons for fighting, by a stable balance of military power that was made easier to maintain by the fact that there were only two major powers to balance against each another and each of them had nuclear weapons.[6] Variations of the Soviet-American relationship have recurred throughout history, an important—some would say the only reliable—source of international tranquillity.

A balance of power is preferable to constant war, but as a method of organizing relations among sovereign states it has its disadvantages. It takes a toll: economically, through the constant preparations for war that it requires; psychologically, because of the insecurity and suspicion involved. It is uncertain. It is based on a particular distribution of military power, but this changes over time, through the slow, steady shift in the distribution of the economic power on which military power ultimately rests[7] and occasionally through sudden, unpredictable breakthroughs in military technology or strategy.

If world government is not feasible and the balance of power less than ideal, the question arises: Is there yet a third way, more feasible than international political hierarchy and more stable and less taxing than international military equilibrium? There is, and the term used here to describe it is common security,[8] the theory and practice of which is the subject of the rest of part II of *The Dawn of Peace in Europe*.

Common security has two defining features. The first is the absence of state-level causes of conflict. The motives for fighting that are rooted in domestic politics are gone. No state wants anything that it regards war as an effective or legitimate method of obtaining. This historically unprecedented circumstance does not, as has been emphasized, abolish all causes of war. The system-level "defensive" cause remains, the insecurity that stems from the international anarchy. While none may wish to fight, each will have to be concerned that others might wish to do so—even if all say they do not. (In the second half of the twentieth century all governments came routinely to declare themselves to be peace-loving, whether or not they actually were.) The potential for a tragedy of misunderstanding, for an unintended but mutually reinforcing "spiral" of hostility, would remain.

Thus the second feature of common security: the recognition of the fact of anarchy and the potential for conflict to which it gives rise, leading to concrete measures to address it. Even if the age-old motives for war are gone, the possibility of war will remain. As long as national independence persists, each state must be concerned about both the intentions and capabilities of others. Each will have to ask: What is the evidence that state-level causes of conflict, the domestic sources of aggression, are extinguished? And, because domestic politics and the motives rooted in them can change, each will also have to ask: How dangerous are others' military forces if state-level causes should, for whatever reason, reemerge?*

Thus there does exist a third way between a balance of power and world government, a method of organizing

---

*The term common security first came into prominent usage in the report of the "Independent Commission on Disarmament and Security Issues," *Common Security: A Blueprint for Survival* (New York: Simon and Schuster, 1983). The group was better known as the Palme Commission, after its chairman, Swedish prime minister Olof Palme. The common security order in place in Europe bears some resemblance to what the Palme Commission recommended: It arises from the recognition that cooperation in setting national levels of armaments is an alternative to a balance of power as a route to security. The Palme Commission, however, was very much a product of the Cold War, its report designed to accommodate the Soviet Union. Thus, unlike the post-Cold War common security order, the commission's recommendations stressed nuclear rather than nonnuclear armaments. Its report included a number of provisions concerning the Third World, which is not relevant to the common security order of the 1990s. The most important difference of all is that the report omitted entirely the domestic component of common security. It did not say that common security requires that participating governments lack aggressive designs on their neighbors. At the time the report was issued the Soviet Union was occupying several of its neighbors.

relations among the major powers that mitigates the effects of anarchy. But is this possible? Is common security, as defined here, any more feasible than world government? Is it possible, is it even conceivable, that all the old familiar motives, the ancient, enduring state-level "offensive" causes of war could ever die out? Is it possible that all the things that people in organized political communities have wanted, and have been willing to fight to get, could cease to be relevant to the calculations of the powerful? The history of international relations is the history of wars fought for gold, God, ground, and glory. Could such wars come to an end?

That question, and some answers to it, also form a chapter in the modern history of ideas about international politics. It concerns the relationship between liberal economic policies—free trade—and liberal political practices—democracy—on the one hand, and peace on the other. Its premise is that the realist perspective is wrong: International behavior varies according to the domestic features of sovereign states; the more liberal they are domestically, the more peaceful will be their international conduct.[9]

In the nineteenth century, British proponents of free trade asserted that because it brought economic benefits, once established it would generate powerful incentives not to disrupt it and forfeit them. War would disrupt trade; thus the more open the trade between countries, the less likely was war between them.[10]

The idea that democracy promotes peace is identified with Immanuel Kant, who proposed it in his 1795 essay "Perpetual Peace,"[11] and with Woodrow Wilson, whose hopes for peace after World War I rested on the spread of democracy.[12] War, both Kant and Wilson reasoned, is contrary to the interests of most citizens of every country.[13] If the public were free to influence government policy everywhere, war would cease. The great barrier to international conflict, Wilson in particular believed, was public opinion. The universal reign of the form of government in which the public and its opinions are sovereign—democracy—would put a stop to the armed conflict that had plagued humankind throughout its largely undemocratic history.

The evidence of the twentieth century suggests that while associating trade and democracy with peace is plausible, the connection has not been proven beyond a reasonable doubt. Growing economic interdependence in Europe at the outset of the twentieth century did not, contrary to some contemporaneous predictions, prevent a major European conflict. After World War II the most deliberate effort to underwrite peace with economic cooperation—the relationship between Germany and France—has succeeded; but this is not the result of economics alone. Both countries were members of an alliance formed to resist a common adversary.

As for liberal politics, here the record does show that full-fledged democracies seldom fight one another, although given the long history of recorded conflict and the shorter history of democratic politics the sample is not a large one.[14] The world has not been a perpetually peaceful place in this or any previous century, but the evidence suggests that this is less because democracies are insufficiently peaceful than because the world has been insufficiently democratic. It is reasonable to conclude that the prospects for common security are enhanced to the extent that the countries in question are democratic, because common security involves the disappearance of state-level causes of war; and democracy seems, on both logical and historical grounds, to be the form of government least susceptible to such causes.[15]

It is here that abstract considerations about the nature of security and the fundamental strategies available for achieving it can be connected to post-Cold War Europe. Europe is not entirely democratic, but it is more democratic than ever before. The least reliably democratic of its major countries, Russia, is central to the future of European security. Because common security depends on the absence of state-level causes of conflict among the major powers, the character of the Russian state is of decisive importance for its prospects, and is the subject of chapter 7.

The future of Russia is crucial, however, for the prospects for *sustaining* common security in post-Cold War Europe, rather than for establishing it, because a common security order in Europe has already been established.

The question of whether the great powers will ever abandon the age-old motives for war, which is the first condition of common security, has been overtaken by events. Common security's second feature, a set of measures designed to reduce as much as possible the insecurity that arises from anarchy, has already come into existence. These measures were put in place in the waning years of the Cold War and in the early part of the post-Cold War period.

In the second half of the twentieth century it became customary for the sovereign states of Europe formally to renounce aggressive intentions. That universal pro forma renunciation is now more credible than ever because of concrete and historically unprecedented steps that have been taken to make it credible. The best evidence for the abandonment of aggressive goals is the voluntary surrender of the means to achieve them. The countries of Europe have done this through a series of arrangements that together constitute a common security order, which is the single most important and least appreciated feature of post-Cold War Europe.

~5~

DEFENSE DOMINANCE

A common security order is a set of arrangements to deal with the cause of international conflict that stems from the underlying anarchy of the international system, which is distinct from the traditional "state-level" causes. The core of the common security order in post-Cold War Europe is the series of arms control accords signed at the end of the Cold War and the outset of the post-Cold War era, beginning with the agreement on Intermediate-Range Nuclear Forces in Europe (INF) in December 1987, and culminating in the second Strategic Arms Reduction Treaty (START II) in January 1993.[1] These arms accords form the heart of a common security order for two reasons.

First, a common security order requires the recognition that anarchy is an independent source of international conflict that will be present even if all the traditional causes disappear. A common security order requires recognizing that, because the structure of the international system itself is the source of the problem of insecurity, all the members of that system must contribute to addressing that problem. All the countries of Europe are parties to the post-1987 arms control accords.[2]

These arms accords are the heart of the common security order for a second reason. Armaments *are* the main system-level cause of conflict. When state-level causes exist, this is not so. Then it is true, as an old saying has it, that nations are not adversaries because they are armed but rather are armed because they are adversaries. Arms are ordinarily the instruments of the political goals for which their possessors are willing to fight.

When there are *no* such goals, however, when the only cause of war is mistaken anxiety about the motives of others, then arms themselves become the cause of conflict because they themselves are what trigger that anxiety. To be sure, arms control agreements per se do not create a common security order. Agreements on nuclear weapons had, after all, been negotiated before 1987: the Limited Test Ban Treaty of 1963, the Nonproliferation Treaty of 1968, and the two Strategic Arms Limitation (SALT) Treaties (the second never formally ratified) of 1972 and 1979. Those earlier agreements did not constitute a common security order. The later ones do because they differ from the earlier accords in crucial ways.

The earlier agreements involved only the Soviet Union and the United States; some of the later ones included all the countries of Europe. Moreover, while the first set of accords included only nuclear weapons, the second set encompassed all the instruments of warfare in Europe including non-nuclear arms. Most importantly, the earlier accords, with the exception of the Antiballistic Missile (ABM) Treaty of 1972, had only marginal effects on the actual military capabilities of the signatories while the later agreements changed their military capacities decisively. The first set of treaties was cosmetic, the second comprehensive.

In fact, although the resemblance between the earlier and later set of agreements is strong on the surface, the two served different purposes because they were created under entirely different political circumstances. The earlier accords were negotiated and signed precisely because the state-level incentives for war were powerful, indeed immutable, on both sides. The United States and the Soviet Union had dramatically different and radically incompatible aspirations for the world and for Europe. If pushed too far, these aspirations could have led to nuclear war, which would have been catastrophic for both countries. Both governments felt the need to signal publicly their joint recognition of this fact, in order to reassure the other and the rest of the world that they understood the dangers of the nuclear age and would keep the political conflict between them from sliding into disaster.[3]

Thus the early arms control accords, which left each country powerfully armed, had a symbolic purpose. They demonstrated that the two rivals could agree on *something*; the terms of agreement, although the subject of intense and protracted negotiation, were less important than the fact that the two governments managed to agree at all. The arms control accords were symbols of a common intention not to wage a particular kind of war, but had virtually no effect on the two sides' capacity to wage that or any other kind of conflict.

The later arms treaties were negotiated under entirely different political conditions and on the basis of the opposite political assumption, that the state-level causes of conflict had all but disappeared.[4] Unlike the earlier agreements, the later accords affected actual military capabilities. Their purpose was not to signal the intention to avoid nuclear war. It was, rather, to convince all of Europe that none of the parties to the accords would wage war of any kind, by reshaping their armed forces so as to make it difficult, if not impossible, to wage aggressive war successfully. The aim, or at least the effect, of these accords was to alleviate the system-level cause of war, the insecurity that anarchy produces.*

The later measures reshaped Europe's military forces according to the principle known as defense dominance: Arms were reduced so as to make them more useful for defending than for attacking. This was partly a matter of which arms were permitted and which were outlawed. It was also a question of numbers, and especially of the end of the numerical asymmetries that had favored the Eastern military bloc. Offensive operations are more difficult and more expensive to conduct than defensive ones, but offense is almost always easier to execute successfully to the extent that the attacker deploys forces numerically superior to those of the defender. The closer to equal the ratio of forces between potential adversaries is—and the late Cold War arms treaties equalized the East-West balance—the less likely a successful attack becomes. Voluntarily accepting force levels that are equal, and thus in most circumstances ill-suited for offensive operations, is a good way for one country to reduce the insecurity of others by signaling that it has no intention of conducting such operations. This was the great accomplishment of the arms treaties of 1987 through 1993.

Nuclear weapons lend themselves to an unusually clear distinction between offense and defense. During the Cold War, a standard for a strictly defensive nuclear posture was established, known as "assured destruction." A country met

---

*This is the basis for what seems at first paradoxical: Arms control was important, it received the most high-level political attention and was at the forefront of the news coverage of international affairs, at a time when it was least important in the sense that its actual impact on military arsenals was modest at best. In fact, there is a logic to the greater prominence of arms control in its earlier than in its later stages: The chance of a nuclear conflict between the United States and the Soviet Union seemed higher in the earlier than in the later period because their political aims were diametrically opposed. It was the end of the political conflict that made possible the extensive military cooperation of the later period.

the requirement for assured destruction when it had a nuclear arsenal that could absorb an all-out attack and still have enough firepower remaining to inflict "unacceptable" damage on the attacker.[5]

If each of two adversaries has a nuclear arsenal that can survive the heaviest assault the other can launch and still do unacceptable damage in return, then assured destruction is mutual. Mutual assured destruction, known by its acronym, "MAD," meets the definition of defense dominance. It does so, ironically, through the superiority of the *offense*. MAD means that, because the attacker in a war cannot evade devastating retaliatory punishment, it cannot win the war. Because the would-be attacker cannot win a war, and knows this in advance, it will not start one. Because this calculation applies to all (or, in the case of the Cold War nuclear standoff, both) parties, none (or neither one) will start a war. When no one starts a war, the result is peace—or, in the term of Cold War discourse, stability.

During the Cold War, assured destruction served as a very rough standard for defining the size and composition of the two major nuclear arsenals. Mutual assured destruction was the logical, unavoidable, although not necessarily desirable (or at least not desired) consequence of the fact that the United States and the Soviet Union each built large, versatile nuclear forces capable of destroying the other even after absorbing a preemptive strike.

The logic of the nuclear confrontation meant that whatever reinforced the condition of mutual assured destruction served defensive purposes, while whatever undermined it—whatever eroded either side's capacity for assured destruction and thereby made an attack by the other potentially advantageous—counted as offensive. During the course of the Cold War, each side mounted a technical challenge to the other's capacity for assured destruction.

The American challenge was a commitment to develop a system of defense against a Soviet nuclear attack. In fact, both countries undertook programs of research on strategic defense almost from the outset of the nuclear age. In 1983, however, President Ronald Reagan made a personal commitment to develop and deploy such a system when he launched the Strategic Defense Initiative (SDI). This was a challenge not only to the fact of mutual assured destruction but also to the treaty that enshrined the principle: the 1972 ABM treaty, negotiated and signed by the United States and the Soviet Union, which effectively prohibited a strategic defense of the kind Reagan proposed. The two countries had agreed to the treaty because, with the stakes so high—the rewards of being the first to mount a succesful defense and the penalties for being second were both so great—without the treaty they would be drawn into a competition in defensive systems that would make each of them poorer and the world less safe. The fact that neither was confident that a working defense system could actually be built served as an added incentive.

Reagan believed that the ABM treaty was technically misconceived, because the United States could ultimately build effective defenses, and morally unacceptable, because the treaty based the nation's safety on a threat—to annihilate its adversary—that it would be immoral to carry out.[6]

Reagan's technological optimism was not borne out. The SDI did not develop an effective system of defense. Constructing a leakproof shield that could be relied upon to prevent *any* of the thousands of nuclear explosives the Soviet Union was capable of launching from striking the continental United States turned out to be a feat of engineering beyond the power of American defense scientists. Because nuclear weapons are so powerful, because just one could level a whole city and kill millions of people, the test of adequacy for strategic defense, unlike for any other weapon in the history of warfare, is perfection. This was a test that no technically feasible system of defense could pass.

The Soviet challenge to the American capacity for assured destruction was less dramatic than SDI but more immediate. The United States never built the system that would have deprived the Soviet Union of assured destruction, but the Soviet Union did deploy weapons that, in the American view, eroded the American capacity to respond to a Soviet attack. Changes in the Soviet fleet of land-based intercontinental ballistic missiles (ICBMs) put the comparable American missiles, by some calculations, at increased risk from a preemptive attack.

Beginning in the 1970s, both sides' missiles were equipped with multiple warheads, known as MIRVs (an acronym for multiple, independently targeted reentry vehicles). At the same time, the guidance systems for missiles improved steadily; they could be fired with ever greater accuracy. As they became more accurate, they posed an increasing threat to the stationary land-based missiles of the other side. A warhead had to land on or very near a missile to destroy or disable it. The more accurate its guidance system, the greater the chance that it would succeed. The chance increased to the extent that one side could aim more than one warhead at a particular missile: The greater the number of warheads aimed at a single target, the greater the chance that one of them would score a direct hit and disable it.

For various reasons, Soviet missiles were larger than American ones and so could carry more warheads. With accuracy on both sides roughly equal, the theoretical advantage belonged to the side with the greater number of warheads available to aim at the other's missiles. Just how great an advantage its larger missiles with more numerous warheads conferred on the Soviet Union, if they conferred any advantage at all, was a matter of debate. The uncertainties surrounding the calculations about a war of land-based missiles was considerable. No Soviet leader was ever likely to be confident that a preemptive strike would incapacitate all of the American land-based missiles. If only a few survived to be fired at the Soviet Union in retaliation, the damage would still be grievous.

Moreover, even if a preemptive strike were perfect, even if it crippled *all* American land-based forces, this would not disarm the United States, which had other nuclear weapons that would survive. The American side could still mount a crushing retaliatory blow by using the other two parts of its strategic nuclear "triad," the nuclear weapons carried by its submarines and its manned bomber aircraft. Even under the most optimistic calculations, the Soviet Union could not hope to win a nuclear war against the United States.

American officials expressed concern, however, that the theoretical possibility of a Soviet advantage in a hypothetical war of land-based missiles would confer a political advantage of some sort. They feared that this hypothetical, technical asymmetry had opened a "window of vulnerability" through which might come unwelcome political consequences. Thus, it became the chief aim of the American side in the ongoing negotiations with the Soviet Union on strategic nuclear weapons to limit Soviet forces in a way that deprived Moscow of its putative advantage in long-range missiles.

In START I and II, signed in 1991 and 1993 respectively, the United States achieved this goal. START I limited each side to a total of 1,600 long-range land- and sea-based ballistic missiles and heavy bombers.[7] Within this overall total, the treaty mandated a 50 percent reduction in the Soviet heavy missiles that Washington regarded as destabilizing. START II went even further: Not only did it stipulate that the nuclear stockpiles on both sides be reduced to within 3,000 and 3,500 warheads over ten years, but also by its terms all multiple warheads on all ballistic missiles were to be eliminated.[8]

The military significance of the START treaties was that by their terms the Soviet advantage in ballistic missiles, whatever the reasons for or consequences of it, disappeared. The treaty enforced the letter of common security—military forces configured for defense, not attack—and implied the Russian acceptance of common security's animating spirit, the recognition that one's own forces can unintentionally be a cause of insecurity, which can spiral into actual conflict.

For American military planners during the Cold War the great nightmare of the nuclear age was a nuclear Pearl Harbor, a sweeping surprise attack on American nuclear forces that would leave the United States vulnerable to the Soviet Union, even as the Japanese attack on December 7, 1941, severely damaged the American Pacific fleet. America's nuclear forces were designed and deployed with the aim of avoiding such a scenario. With START I and II, the United States succeeded in enlisting Soviet and Russian cooperation in this effort.

The two START treaties covered strategic nuclear weapons: those based in one country or at sea and with the capacity to strike targets on the territory of the other. The majority of American and Soviet nuclear weapons were of two other types: those of intermediate range, based in Eastern Europe and capable of reaching Western Europe and vice versa; and tactical nuclear weapons, for use on the battlefield at the heart of Europe, in Germany. Reconfiguring these other categories of nuclear weapons to make them compatible with the principle of assured destruction would have been a more complicated undertaking than the task of doing so for strategic nuclear armaments. The two governments brought the other nuclear weapons into conformity with the principle of defense dominance in a radical way, by eliminating them altogether.

In December 1987, President Reagan and the Soviet leader Mikhail Gorbachev signed a treaty eliminating all 2,611 intermediate-range American and Soviet missiles from Europe.[9] In September 1991, President George Bush announced that all American-controlled land-based and sea-based tactical nuclear weapons would be withdrawn to the United States. The next month Gorbachev responded by ordering similar measures for the comparable Soviet weapons.[10] As a result, Europe became, for the first time in four decades, something very close to a nuclear weapon-free zone.

During the Cold War, this had been a goal of the Soviet Union. The non-nuclear forces of the Soviet-dominated Warsaw Pact were presumed to be more powerful than those of NATO,[11] an advantage that was offset by nuclear parity. If nuclear weapons were removed, the uneven non-nuclear balance would become more important. Like the window of vulnerability in strategic nuclear weapons, it was feared that the denuclearization of Europe leading to the increased salience of the non-nuclear imbalance between East and West, even if it did not produce a direct attack on NATO forces, would work to the political disadvantage of the West.

When the final nuclear weapons were removed from Europe, however, the imbalance in non-nuclear arms no longer concerned the West. In the interim, it had been corrected by another treaty, which concerned Conventional Forces in Europe (CFE). The effect of the CFE accord was to restructure non-nuclear armaments on both sides to bring them into conformity with the principles of defense dominance, just as START I and START II had done with strategic nuclear forces.

While the two sides had concluded several agreements on nuclear weapons before the START treaties, and one of them, the 1972 ABM treaty, contributed to the defense dominance that is integral to common security, prior to 1990 the two military blocs had never agreed on limits to non-nuclear, or "conventional" weaponry.[12] They had made one serious effort to do so in the 1970s, the talks on Mutual and Balanced Force Reductions, which ended in stalemate.[13]

The CFE treaty was more complicated than either START I or START II. The two military coalitions had many more conventional than nuclear weapons, and they came in different shapes and sizes, with diverse military purposes. Moreover, while nuclear weapons involved only the United States and the Soviet Union, conventional force negotiations were the business of all the countries of Europe and North America. Conventional weapons differed from nuclear armaments as well because they were more closely related to actual political purposes. By the last decade of the Cold War there was a consensus on both sides of the East-West divide that, as President Reagan put it, "nuclear war cannot be won and must never be fought." There was no such consensus about conventional weapons.[14] They served one particular purpose for the Soviet Union that the United States did not share. Soviet troops stationed in Eastern Europe were the ultimate mechanism for controlling the countries of the region. Moscow may have calculated that diluting its military presence would weaken its political grip.*

The terms of the CFE treaty favored defense over offense in two related ways. First, the treaty placed limits on military equipment useful for attack: tanks, airplanes, artillery pieces, and troops—the instruments of modern

---

*In the end things worked the other way around: First the Communist regime collapsed, then the Soviet forces withdrew. Christopher Jones has argued that the Warsaw Pact was configured for offensive operations not primarily because Moscow planned to attack westward but rather because this military strategy lent itself to a pattern of military organization that maximized Soviet political control. Offensive operations require not only larger but also integrated forces. Thus, during the Cold War, Eastern European forces were controlled by Soviet commanders. If the Warsaw Pact's military mission had been simply to defend territory, it could have been carried out by national armies unconnected with one another, which would, however, have given the Communist governments of Eastern Europe, by controlling their own armed forces, a measure of leverage against Moscow. The Communist government of Romania, which did control its own military forces, did achieve a degree of independence from Moscow in foreign policy. Christopher Jones, *Soviet Influence in Eastern Europe: Political Autonomy and the Warsaw Pact* (New York: Praeger, 1981).

combined-arms non-nuclear combat.[15] Second, it mandated equal totals for the opposing military coalitions. Because the Warsaw Pact forces were more numerous, this made for sharper reductions on the Communist side. They were required to reduce their forces by 130,000 items. By contrast, in order to reach the common ceiling the West needed to eliminate only a few thousand weapons.[16]

This second feature had political significance: Because it required actual reductions and because the Warsaw Pact had to make larger reductions than NATO did, the treaty was popular in the West, particularly in the United States. Numerical equality had a strategic as well as a political significance. Equality favors the defensive side because, as noted, in warfare a successful offensive campaign ordinarily requires numerical supremacy. An often-cited rule of thumb is that a three-to-one advantage is necessary for a successful attack. It was the numerical superiority of the Warsaw Pact rather than the quality of its equipment, training, or morale (which were all inferior to those of the West) on which had rested the Western judgment that the conventional balance favored the Communist side. The CFE treaty eliminated that superiority.

To be sure, there were loopholes in the CFE treaty. It covered only the territory of the former Soviet Union to the western edge of the Ural Mountains. During the summer and fall of 1990, in anticipation that the treaty would be signed, the then-Soviet military "was estimated to have moved nearly 60,000 treaty-limited pieces of equipment, including enough tanks for fifty heavy armed tank divisions, beyond the Urals, out of the CFE area of application and out of treaty coverage. . . ."[17]

Nor were all weapons in Europe covered by the treaty. Naval and strategic rocket forces were excluded. The Soviet side asserted that some armaments that were obviously geared to ground warfare were in fact part of the Soviet navy.[18] And the reductions were perhaps not as well tailored as they might have been to the task of reshaping the armies of Europe for defensive rather than offensive purposes. They permitted, for example, a considerable number of combat aircraft.[19]

Still, a series of supplementary commitments strengthened the limits on offensive forces.[20] More importantly, political developments after the November 1990 signing of the CFE treaty weakened Russia militarily, further reducing its potential for offensive operations and thus reinforcing common security in Europe. Foremost among these developments was the disintegration of the Soviet Union and the emergence of successor states possessing weapons covered by the CFE treaty. This great political earthquake, while reducing Russian military potential, could also have posed enormous problems of revision and implementation for the treaty. Fortunately, the way it had been negotiated provided the basis for resolving such problems. During the negotiations France had insisted on including national subtotals within the overall bloc limits. This made it possible for the successor states to the Soviet Union to divide among themselves the armaments covered by CFE that they had inherited. This they did in an agreement signed in Tashkent, in newly independent Uzbekistan, in May 1992.[21]

The Tashkent accords reinforced the constraints on the offensive military potential of Russia, the only one of the Soviet successor states likely to threaten the peace of Europe. For example, the treaty permitted Russia only 6,400 tanks west of the Urals; NATO countries were entitled, by the terms of the CFE treaty, to a total of 20,000.[22]

In fact, the great political upheavals of 1989 and 1991 moved the line of potential conflict in Europe—the place where a major European war was likeliest to erupt—almost a thousand miles to the east. It was no longer the cease-fire line of World War II, which ran through the middle of Germany. Instead, it became the border between Russia and Ukraine.[23]

During the Cold War, the Western military planners' nightmare for conventional weapons, the equivalent of a "nuclear Pearl Harbor," was a repetition by Soviet-led military forces in the center of Germany of the German blitzkrieg attack on France in May 1940. The Wehrmacht's sudden strike westward pierced the French line of defense, leading to the rout of the French army, a German sweep to the English Channel, and the occupation of most of France, all in six weeks. The CFE treaty not only moved eastward the point from which Russia would have to launch such an attack, but it also severely restricted Russia's complement of the arms needed to execute it.

The treaty-imposed restrictions on arms did not by themselves constitute a common security order, which also requires universal confidence that the limits are being observed and that no country can attack another even while observing them. Such confidence was supplied by another feature of the negotiated agreements between East and West: the principle that every country is entitled to see what weapons all the others actually have and what they are doing with them. That principle is known as transparency.

~6~

CONFIDENCE BUILDING

Common security depends on addressing the system-level cause of war, which, when state-level causes have disappeared, is embodied in weapons. The post-1987 arms control accords were designed to ease the insecurity that anarchy produces by imposing limits reconfiguring Europe's nuclear and non-nuclear armaments to make them suitable for defense but not attack. Easing insecurity requires the existence not only of such limits but also of confidence among all parties that the others are observing the limits.

There is another, related requirement, stemming from the fact that the difference between offense and defense, while crucial in principle, is not always clear in practice. Weapons cannot always be definitively categorized as one or the other. In premodern warfare the distinction was sometimes readily apparent: Fortifications were obviously designed for defense; catapults and battering rams were for offense. Modern military forces, however, are less clearly designed for either attack or resistance. The countries of

Europe cannot be absolutely certain that the arms their neighbors are permitted to have, even under the terms of the treaties of 1987 to 1993, can never be used to attack them.

To address these two related problems, the later arms control accords have, in addition to defense dominance, a second distinguishing feature: transparency. Transparency means that each country can be confident both that none of the others has weapons that are forbidden to it and that no country is preparing to use for offensive purposes the arms it does possess legally.

Transparency was part of the early Soviet-American arms control accords. The United States had insisted that it be able to verify compliance by the Soviet Union, a country that was a closed society with a history, at least in the American view, of repudiating or cheating on international agreements into which it had entered. Therefore, it became an unshakable American precept of Cold War arms negotiations that treaties could encompass only weapons that could reliably be verified. Because the Soviet government kept virtually all information about military matters secret, verification was accomplished by means of photographs taken by high-resolution cameras mounted on reconnaissance satellites that both countries regularly launched.

It was thus the technical capabilities of satellite photography that set the limits on the scope of arms control agreements: What could clearly and reliably be photographed from space could be counted; what could be counted could be verified; what could be verified could be limited by treaty. Because, before 1987, strategic nuclear weapons could be reliably monitored and weapons of other kinds could not be, it was only strategic nuclear weapons that were limited by treaty.

In September 1986, a breakthrough occurred. At a meeting of the Conference on Security and Cooperation in Europe (CSCE) in Stockholm the Soviet government agreed for the first time to permit "on-site inspection" by Western personnel.

Previously Western inspectors had had to pore over satellite photographs to verify Soviet compliance with arms accords. The treaty on Intermediate-Range Nuclear Forces (INF) of the following year permitted representatives of each side to witness the other dismantling the weapons the destruction of which the treaty required. Because it would have been impossible to track by satellite all the forces it covered, the landmark CFE treaty of 1990 would have been impossible without its unprecedented provisions for on-site inspection.

The beginning of on-site inspection was a watershed event in East-West relations because it made possible arms control agreements broad enough to serve as the basis of a common security order in Europe. The post-1987 arms accords differed from the earlier ones in permitting more intrusive inspection, and thus more extensive limitations on arms, including, for the first time, non-nuclear weapons.

There is a second, related, and equally important difference between the earlier and the later accords. The later ones, in particular those involving conventional weapons, limited not only what military forces each country could have, but also how each could use them. Numerical limits cannot by themselves eliminate the danger of a latter-day blitzkrieg attack. France had more tanks than did Germany in 1940: The German attack succeeded because the German army was able to concentrate its tanks at a particular point on the line of confrontation between the two countries. This was possible because Germany took France by surprise. The French commanders did not know the location of the German tank formations. Defense dominance therefore requires limits not only on what forces a country has but also on how they can be used—including when and where they can be moved—in order to prevent a successful surprise attack. The later arms treaties included such limits.

The provisions to prevent a successful surprise attack, even by a country whose overall forces are not more numerous than those of its adversary, fall into three categories.

One is the continuous surveillance of all military forces through both satellite reconnaissance and on-site inspection: All European governments can know at all times not only what military forces all the others have but also what the others are doing with them. The second is prenotification. If training maneuvers in Europe involve forces above a certain size, the country undertaking them is required to give public notice of these maneuvers well in advance. The third actually prohibits military maneuvers, even for training purposes, of forces beyond certain numerical limits.

These restraints, all intended to convey the assurance that surprise attack is impossible, are called Confidence Building Measures (CBMs). They grew out of a series of East-West negotiations between 1986 and 1992. They began during the Cold War, in 1975, as part of the Helsinki Accords signed that year. A more comprehensive set of CBMs than Helsinki produced was authorized in Stockholm in 1986, paving the way for further measures agreed to at Paris in 1990 and Vienna in 1992.[1] The measures became progressively restrictive: The time required between the notification of a maneuver and the maneuver itself lengthened; the size of the maneuvers that had to be announced in advance and the limits beyond which any maneuver, no matter how clearly announced as such, was impermissible, were lowered.*

CBMs were not only an important part of the common security order, but are also a metaphor for common security

---

*CBMs emerged from negotiations conducted under the auspices of the Conference on Security and Cooperation in Europe (CSCE), which was established at Helsinki in 1975. The success of these negotiations gave rise to the hope that the CSCE could serve as a new pan-European security organization, a hope expressed by the decision to change its name to the *Organization* for Security and Cooperation in Europe (OSCE). In practice, this meant serving as a Europe-wide police force, a role it could not play for the same reason that the stronger, more cohesive, and better established NATO was unable to do so: the absence of a common European conscience itself. For the ultimate purpose of common security is to promote confidence in the peaceful intentions of others. A common security order is successful to the extent that all parties to it have confidence that none will be attacked by any other. Restraints on military forces that make attack unlikely are the basis for such confidence. If all countries voluntarily surrender the *capability* for attack, each can reasonably, with confidence, infer that no other harbors any *motive* for attacking. Arms limits of the kind enacted in 1987 and thereafter are a sign that state-level causes of war are at least in remission in Europe. The renunciation of certain capabilities, that is, is a measure of intentions. Asked once whether he would be a candidate for the presidency, former New York governor Mario Cuomo replied that he had no plans to run and no plans to make plans. Transparency conveys a similar message for security in Europe. The information available because of the verification clauses of the arms control treaties and the terms of the CBMs provides assurance that no state has plans for war; the fact that such information is available on an ongoing basis, its supply assured by sworn treaties, is itself reassuring evidence that no state has plans to make such plans.

Moreover, of the two components of defense dominance embodied in the arms treaties and the CBMs, one, the renunciation of offensive military maneuvers, reinforces the other, the relinquishing of offensive military capabilities.

The fact of renunciation is important in and of itself. Strictly speaking, the promise not to undertake offensive

---

and a common European will. There was no consensus among the membership of the OSCE, which was larger and far more heterogeneous than that of NATO, about the norms to be enforced in Europe. Nor was there a consensus within each member country on the desirability of contributing military forces to enforce such norms, even if Europe-wide agreement on them could be reached. On NATO's shortcomings as a European police force see chapter 2.

military maneuvers that could turn into combat operations is not necessary to prevent surprise attack. Satellite monitoring has made it virtually impossible to conduct large-scale maneuvers in Europe undetected, regardless of whether these maneuvers are announced in advance. Like a giant department store continuously monitored by video cameras covering every part of the sales floor to detect shoplifting, the European continent has become transparent by dint of reconnaissance satellites, all apart from any treaties promoting the exchange of information. Agreements legalizing this monitoring are significant because, by agreeing to provide notice and to renounce maneuvers beyond a certain scale, all parties are in effect agreeing to define activities outside these restraints as *illegal*. This reinforces the likelihood of successful defense against surprise attack. In modern times, such attacks have typically succeeded not because the defending country did not know the attack was imminent but rather because it was unable to make the *political* decision to mobilize in time to thwart the attack.

Ambiguity, wishful thinking, and internal political conflicts based on differing interpretations of events have often produced paralysis in the face of imminent threat, thereby blocking an effective response to what was, in fact, aggression. The problem, as the most authoritative study of the issue has observed, is not detection but decision, not intelligence failure but political disbelief.[2] With officially recognized limits on military maneuvers, violations become unambiguous acts of aggression, reducing the chance of the uncertainty and hesitation that have paved the way for successful surprise attacks in the past.

During the Cold War, NATO was trained, equipped, and deployed to meet, but not to launch, a surprise attack. As the danger of this scenario receded, the alliance adapted. With a few modest adjustments and without changing its basic structure, NATO has become part of the common security order. Although no longer central to the new security arrangements in the way that it was to the bipolar standoff of the Cold War, NATO remains relevant and important to European security. Its continued existence was presumed when the arms control accords at the heart of the new security regime were negotiated. Treaty-limited weapons were allocated to NATO countries, including the United States, a European power by virtue of its membership in the Atlantic Alliance. In particular, the United States is central to the accords involving nuclear weapons, as the designated possessor of all the treaty-limited Western nuclear arms. The transparency that is crucial for common security, moreover, is made possible in large measure by the surveillance technology of the United States. American satellites monitor the levels and the movements of the armed forces of Europe.

Furthermore, in adapting itself to the post-Cold War era, NATO has itself become a kind of CBM. In 1991 it established the North Atlantic Cooperation Council (NACC), in which former members of the Warsaw Pact could participate.[3] The NACC's function is the same as the CBMs negotiated under CSCE auspices: to promote transparency.

NATO's Partnership for Peace was established in 1993 for the same purpose. Non-members were invited to work out individual programs of military cooperation with the Atlantic Alliance. The significance of these programs lies not in any joint task that they involve, such as peacekeeping, but in reassurance about intentions and capabilities that the process of interaction engenders. Among former adversaries, familiarity of this kind, its participants hope, will breed not contempt but confidence.

NATO is a source of confidence in yet another way, as insurance in the event of the failure of common security. If the common security order collapses, if Europe again becomes a dangerous place, the Western Europeans can be confident that the political structure on which their security rested when conditions were similar, during the Cold War, will remain in place. NATO as a CBM addresses the system-level cause of conflict, providing reassurance that no one will launch an attack. NATO as a continuing defensive alliance offers protection in the event of the reappearance of state-level causes of war.

To summarize: Common security requires that all countries demonstrate that they recognize the existence of a system-level cause of war, anarchy, which persists even after state-level causes are in abeyance. The arms control accords of 1987 to 1993 have accomplished this because all the countries of Europe are party to them, denoting a common understanding of the need for measures to make benign intentions credible to others. Common security requires not only the recognition of the general problem of insecurity but also concrete steps to address its cause: The arms control accords of 1987 to 1993 have eased Europe's chronic insecurity by reshaping the continent's military forces and regulating their operations according to the principles of defense dominance and transparency.

Common security does not make war impossible. It does not establish an enforceable international legal regime with its own government and police force. But it does as much as can be done in the absence of international government to reduce the possibility of great-power conflict. The nations of Europe can have confidence that, as long as the elements of the common security order endure, there will be no major war in Europe. This is a remarkable diplomatic achievement and a dramatic change. Yet it has gone largely unappreciated, indeed, as an historic innovation in the arrangements for security in Europe, largely unrecognized. What accounts for this?

One reason is that the establishment of its centerpiece, the arms treaties, was overshadowed by the monumental political changes of which those treaties were both harbingers and consequences. The fall of communism in Europe was a spectacular series of events: unexpected, startling, revolutionary. The arms accords were also, in their own way, revolutionary, but less obviously so. They look familiar. They seem to continue the superpower routines of the Cold War era, although they depart from the earlier patterns in fundamental ways.[4]

There is another, related reason that the new common security order has not received its due. The arms agreements, along with the fall of Communist governments from Berlin to Vladivostok and the emergence of new independent states on the territory of the former Soviet Union (and of two other Communist multinational states, Yugoslavia and Czechoslovakia), form the post-Cold War peace settlement. Together they comprise the functional equivalent of what emerged from the Congress of Vienna of 1815, which was convened after the Napoleonic Wars, the Paris Peace Conference of 1919 after World War I, and the Yalta and Potsdam conferences of 1945, the closest approximations of a peace conference for World War II.

If the arms treaties and political developments of 1987 through 1993 are equivalent in function to the settlements following the previous wars, however, they are not equivalent in form. They have been less noticed because they are less noticeable. No dramatic post-Cold War peace conference was convened. No single, comprehensive document reordering Europe was negotiated. Nor did the post-Cold War settlement produce a commanding figure like Metternich in 1815, Wilson in 1919, or the big three—Roosevelt, Churchill, and Stalin—in 1945. There is a grand design to the settlement—common security—but no grand designer. Nor was there a single moment when the European settlement was put in place. The post-Cold War settlement is like the English rather than the American constitution: It is not the result of a single dramatic deliberation. Instead, it emerged piece by piece, over time.

Moreover, the common security order has an odd pedigree. It is the product of an unrecognized and entirely unintended three-way collaboration among the German left, the

American right, and what passed, in the dying days of the USSR, for the Soviet center.

It was politicians on the German left who first gave public prominence to the idea of defense dominance, which they called "defensive defense." They insisted on the difference in practice between military forces useful for attack and those appropriate for defense. They wanted their own country, the German Federal Republic, and NATO, to adopt a purely defensive military posture. Their goal was to set aside and thus overcome the political differences at the heart of the East-West conflict. They wanted to end that conflict by creating a "security partnership," if not between the rival military blocs then at least between the two Germanies.[5]

The idea of defense dominance was adopted as the basis for practical policy by someone pursuing the opposite goal: President Ronald Reagan. He wanted to win the conflict that the German left wanted to set aside. He believed that the asymmetries between NATO and the Warsaw Pact in nuclear and conventional weaponry were of benefit to the Communist bloc. He therefore presided over the drafting of Western arms control proposals that sought to eliminate them. He believed that the Western governments should base their negotiating positions not on what was merely feasible but on what was desirable.

Because equality at lower levels of weapons required considerably larger reductions by the Communist side, critics of the Reagan arms control policies considered his approach to be a recipe for stalemate, a way of ensuring that no agreements would ever be concluded. "Any administration that thinks that it can get the Soviets to take down two-thirds or more of their most modern and powerful missiles," one of the critics remarked in the early 1980s, "should also be asking for the restoration of the Romanov dynasty and the establishment of Judaism as the state religion."[6]

A decade later, while the Romanovs seemed no nearer to regaining power and a large number of Soviet Jews had moved to Israel, a treaty stipulating the destruction of *all* of those missiles had been signed. This was the accomplishment of Mikhail Gorbachev. The European left developed the ideas of common security for one reason; Ronald Reagan introduced them into American negotiating positions for a different, contrary reason; and Gorbachev accepted those proposals for yet a third reason. His motive was the opposite of Reagan's. He sought to strengthen, not weaken the Soviet Union.[7] He was convinced that this required the economic renewal of the country, which, he concluded, was possible only through a sharp reduction of the burden of defense spending. This, he decided, could best be achieved by arms reductions in cooperation with the West.

In addition to its quiet, piecemeal development and its unusual political pedigree, there is yet a third reason for the relative obscurity of the new common security order. As a principle of international order, common security lacks the clarity and simplicity, as well as the familiarity, of the two alternatives—world government and the balance of power. Its claims are more modest. It does not solve, once and for all, the problem of conflict in Europe. It can be understood not as a formula for abolishing war but rather as a method of buying time. Time contributes to the confidence that common security engenders in two ways.

First, a would-be European aggressor would need time to overcome the restrictions on the forces necessary for attack imposed by the common security order. Once having accepted and incorporated these restrictions, a country bent on overturning the European status quo could not hope to mount a successful attack without extensive preparations, which would be readily detected and would plainly violate signed treaties. One effect of common security is to extend the warning time for an attack in Europe from the minutes of the Cold War to the years that would be required in the post-Cold War era to organize an effective offensive capacity.

Time builds confidence in a second way. Over time, as common security arrangements persist, they become more familiar, reliable, and credible. This engenders confidence in their durability. If limits and restrictions have held in the past, this is evidence that they will hold in the future.

A common security order does not do the work of a standing police force. It does not end all strife in Europe. It is not a solution to future Bosnias. But it is a solution to what has been the most serious problem in European history, the problem to which NATO expansion is claimed by its advocates to respond, the problem of great-power conflict. Indeed, as long as the common security order holds, it will accomplish what NATO expansion cannot: It will include Russia while reassuring the countries of Central and Eastern Europe. It offers the prospect of making all Europeans secure without drawing a new line of division among them, as NATO expansion would.

Like the other possible futures for NATO and European security, common security has an historical antecedent. It incorporates some of the features of postwar European security arrangements that, from the perspective of the close of the twentieth century, are the most distant and obscure. These arrangements, which followed the Napoleonic Wars and were known as the Concert of Europe, formed what was arguably the most successful postwar European settlement.[8]

The Concert of Europe was a set of informal understandings according to which, in the wake of the Napoleonic Wars, the European great powers acted collectively to defuse problems that might lead to conflict among them. They did so by convening conferences at which solutions to those problems were hammered out. Several such conferences were held in the decade following the war. Toward the end of the nineteenth century, in 1878, and in the early years of the twentieth, in 1908 and 1913, the same procedure was employed to pacify quarrels in the Balkans.

Balkan conflict was not, however, finally settled, and it ultimately triggered the next great European war in 1914, bringing to a close the century during which the Concert of Europe had operated.

The common security order is similar to the Concert of Europe in that both are informal arrangements, not formal organizations, although each included formal treaties. The two are similar as well in that both adopted a collective approach to security problems, involving all the most powerful European states. Implicit in both was the understanding that security is a common problem, to which common responses are therefore advantageous. A third similarity is that the version of the general problem of security that both were created to address was significant but specific: to prevent a general war. Neither was designed to stamp out all instability or impose any particular definition of justice throughout Europe. Neither was intended to prevent all wars, just a major war.*

As with the other post-Cold War approaches to European security, its historical antecedent offers a cautionary lesson for the future of common security. In the past,

---

*The Concert of Europe was based on the presumption that the familiar state-level causes of war would persist. At the outset of the nineteenth century it was unthinkable that the great powers would ever give up the quest for power, prestige, wealth, and above all for territory—which was presumed to be the source of the other three. The common security order of the 1990s rests on the opposite presumption, that the age-old incentives for states to go to war in order to become bigger, richer, and more powerful have, for whatever reason, all but died out among the major powers of Europe.

War on the scale of the Napoleonic conflicts was seen as dangerous by the political leaders of post-Napoleonic Europe because it could unleash political forces—nationalism and liberalism—that would threaten them personally, since these leaders ruled multinational empires, not nation-states. The Concert of Europe was thus organized to stifle precisely those political currents the triumph of which, with the collapse of communism, made common security feasible.

the obstacle to perpetuating the winning coalition, the desire for which is reflected in the widespread post-Cold War interest in retaining NATO, was the wish of one of its members to withdraw from European affairs.[9] The idea of a European police force, reincarnated in the post-Cold War era in the proposal that NATO adopt out-of-area missions, failed for lack of agreement among the great powers on how peripheral conflicts should be settled and on the urgency of settling them. The effort to contain the defeated power, the purpose of NATO expansion, misfired after World War I when it served to provoke Germany, contributing to a renewed German campaign of conquest. So, too, the Concert of Europe ended in a way that is relevant to the post-Cold War common security order.

Both were not only collective systems, including all the major powers, but voluntary as well. No superior power enforced the norms each embodied. The Concert of Europe was, and the post-Cold War common security order is, a form of world order without world government. Thus, each party was and is free not to follow its rules. Any party could and can "defect"; and defection destroys the entire arrangement in both cases. Unanimity is a necessary condition for common security: Either every country enjoys its benefits or none does.

The general European peace, or at least the freedom from a major, protracted war, which lasted for a century after 1815, was destroyed by the defection of one of the major powers. Imperial Germany became so impatient with the status quo in 1914 that it was willing to start a war on the scale of the Napoleonic conflict, one that drew in all the other great powers and ultimately the United States, to overturn that status quo.

The common security order is similarly vulnerable. If any major European country should decide to withdraw, it would collapse. In that case, Europe would again become an arena for interstate rivalry, in which the only available mechanism for peace would be a balance of power. The like-liest potential defector, the major power whose commitment to common security is shakiest, is Russia. The future of the common security order, a new, superior, and unprecedented set of arrangements for European security, therefore depends on the political future of Europe's largest country.

~Part III~

THE SUPERPOWERS

~7~

THE RUSSIAN REGIME

In 1947 George Kennan published an article in the quarterly journal *Foreign Affairs* entitled "The Sources of Soviet Conduct," which established the intellectual foundations for American foreign policy during the Cold War. His argument was straightforward: The Soviet Union was bound to be hostile to the West because the Communist system made rivalry unavoidable. The Soviet leaders' need to maintain total power within the country led them to designate a dangerous, implacable enemy outside its gates: world capitalism. Internal Soviet politics determined external behavior in a clear, predictable, unalterable way: Communism was, per se, a state-level cause of conflict.

The security of Europe depends on the future of the largest successor state of the Soviet Union: Russia. The Russian question after the Cold War is as important for the future of European security as the Soviet question after World War II, although it is more complicated. While the ebb and flow of Russian politics is relevant and the outcome of particular elections important, it is the character of the

Russian regime itself that is crucial. The prospects for common security depend on Russian foreign policy, which depends in part on what kind of Russia conducts it. While after World War II the political system was fixed, with Stalin and communism firmly installed in power from Vladivostok to the middle of Germany, now it is uncertain, in flux.

Kennan's analysis of the Soviet regime was intended to supply what the West lacked: a policy toward the Soviet Union. In the wake of the Cold War the West has a clear and promising approach: a series of policies consistent with common security. What is in question is whether Russia will continue to be the kind of country that will participate in the common security order. Five years after the collapse of the Soviet Union, the range of choices before Russia was unusually wide, the result of its size, traditions, and location. Poland, another formerly Communist European country, is part of the West—by choice, by geography, and because it is not large or distant enough to resist the political, ideological, economic, and cultural influences of Western Europe. None of that is true of Russia.

The difference between the post-World War II Soviet Union and post-Cold War Russia is the difference between a secret (something that some know and others do not) and a mystery (something that no one knows).[1] The Soviet Union about which Kennan wrote was secretive. While the details of Kremlin politics were hidden, however, the consequences for the West, according to Kennan, were predictable: Stalin was a reliable international figure, reliably hostile. Post-Cold War Russia, by contrast, is mysterious; its continued fidelity to the spirit and the letter of the common security order is in doubt because its political future is unknown.

The strongest guarantee that a country will adhere to the norms of common security is an understanding of common security's logic, the acceptance of its principles, and the conviction that it offers the optimal method of safeguarding the country's own security.

Mikhail Gorbachev, the person most responsible for Russian membership in the post-Cold War European security order, seems to have been motivated by conviction. To be sure, the overall policy of which common security was a part—conciliation with the West—was intended to assist the revitalization of the Soviet Union by easing the burden of military competition. Gorbachev's ultimate concern was the vitality of his own country, not the security of Europe.[2] Still, what he said about European security suggested that he understood and even embraced the tenets of common security. One of his contributions to the official Soviet ideology was what came to be called the "new thinking" on foreign policy, which consisted largely of the precepts of common security.

Gorbachev asserted that security had to be achieved in common, rather than unilaterally: Security, he said, "can only be mutual . . ."[3] It involved "the recognition of others' interests."[4] The imperative of the age was that "adversaries must become partners and start looking jointly for a way to achieve universal security."[5]

This meant that security could not be achieved solely by military means and that "attempts to achieve military superiority are preposterous."[6] Indeed, the Soviet Union would not want changes in the strategic balance in its own favor, he said, because this would bestow no lasting advantage but instead "strengthen suspicion and increase instability."[7] Soviet security would in fact be enhanced by dispelling "unwarranted but not inexplicable Western fears."[8]

The implication of this reasoning was that military doctrines "should be strictly doctrines of defense. And this is connected with such new or comparatively new notions as the reasonable sufficiency of armaments, non-aggressive defense, the elimination of disbalance and asymmetries in various types of armed forces . . ."[9] Gorbachev conceded that this would require changes in the force postures in Europe, including changes in the forces he himself controlled: "There

are imbalances and asymmetries in some kinds of armaments and armed forces on both sides in Europe . . . We
stand for eliminating the inequality existing in some areas,
but not through a build-up by those who lag behind but
through a reduction by those who are ahead."[10] In a book
published in 1987 he foresaw much of what the arms control
accords of the next six years were to achieve:

> . . . reduction and eventual elimination of the tacti-
> cal nuclear weapons, to be coupled with a drastic
> reduction of the armed forces and conventional
> weapons; withdrawal of offensive weapons from
> direct contact in order to rule out the possibility of
> a surprise attack; and a change in the entire pattern
> of armed forces with a view to imparting an exclu-
> sively defensive character to them.[11]

He endorsed the military concept at the heart of common security: defense dominance. "We believe that armaments should be reduced to the level of reasonable
sufficiency, that is, a level necessary for strictly defensive
purposes. It is time the two military alliances amended their
strategic concepts to gear them more to the aims of defense.
Every apartment in the 'European home' has the right to
protect itself against burglars, but it must do so without
destroying its neighbors' property."[12]

Talk of this sort tends to be cheap. Soviet leaders had
proclaimed their devotion to peace since Stalin's day. But
Gorbachev went further. He explained the underlying rationale for common security, something no previous Soviet
leader had done. He went further still: The late–Cold War
arms accords to which he agreed included concrete steps
that put the principles of common security into practice.

The concepts underlying common security come from
the West. Their origins lie in ideas about politics—the
desirability and feasibility of peace foremost among

them—that are part of the Western liberal tradition. This is a tradition largely alien to Russia. It was neither natural nor predictable that the government of the Communist superpower would adopt them. The Gorbachev era, and thus the figure of Mikhail Gorbachev himself, were probably indispensable for their adoption. The uniquely powerful role of the general secretary of the Communist party of the Soviet Union within the eastern military bloc in combination with Gorbachev's skill at maneuvering within the party made it possible for him, almost alone, to impose on the Soviet empire a radical departure from the traditional Communist and Russian approach to security.

The arms treaties, as well as the decision to withdraw military forces first from Eastern Europe and then from independent countries that had become the western military districts of the Soviet Union, encountered resistance in Russia. These initiatives were opposed by Communist Party officials and by the military.[13]

But the hypercentralized political tradition of communism, the absence of any constitutional checks on the supreme leader, made it possible for Gorbachev to override their objections. Just as the Emperor Constantine brought Christianity to the Roman empire, so Mikhail Gorbachev, with help from only a handful of associates, converted the Soviet empire to common security. He was strong enough domestically to impose security policies that were unfamiliar and unpopular; but at the same time he presided over a country weak enough externally that these policies seemed necessary for its revitalization.

Because Gorbachev was so important, because common security is so sharply at odds with the Russian and Soviet tradition, because only a minority of the Soviet political class was ever persuaded of its intrinsic merits, his fall from power calls into question the durability of the commitments that he made. They are all the more questionable because his downfall occurred under circumstances that created widespread support for a radically different approach to foreign policy.

Gorbachev's downfall coincided with the end of the Soviet Union itself, the Russian core of which surrendered control of territory to the west and south that had been part of the imperial Russian and Soviet states for centuries. This created fertile ground in Russia for feelings of anger, betrayal, resentment, and irredentism.

Five years later, the rhetoric of the new Russian leadership and political class across party lines did not stress the tenets of common security. The thrust of Russian foreign policy toward the West changed from accommodation to estrangement. Strident assertions of Russia's right to a sphere of predominance on the territory of the former Soviet Union, and in some cases farther to the west, became common.[14] Russian foreign policy came to include as well a sense of grievance against the West, which stood accused of conniving to undermine the Soviet Union and destroy Russian power. Gorbachev and Shevardnadze came to be seen in retrospect by many Russians not as visionary co-architects of a new, better, safer European security order, but rather as instigators of a "disorderly retreat and capitulation before the West."[15]

In contrast to Gorbachev's innovations in the conceptual apparatus of foreign policy, this was the oldest of old thinking; and Russian policy toward some of its neighbors went beyond rhetoric. All across its southern border, Moscow intervened in the internal affairs of what were, beginning in 1992, independent countries.[16]

This was not, however, a simple reversal of policy or an outright rejection of common security. The new Russia was dealing with a different international environment, and addressing a different set of intentional issues, than had the Soviet Union. Indeed, Russia was a different country from the old Soviet Union; and for the ultimate prospects of common security, the change was for the better.

In the short term, the abrupt change of tone in the discourse of Russian foreign policy did not doom—although it scarcely reinforced—Russia's commitment to common security. In the longer term, Gorbachev's downfall and its aftermath may well serve to strengthen that commitment. The disappearance of orthodox communism and the tentative construction of democracy are, for this purpose, encouraging developments. Communism is bad and democracy is good for the common security order because both directly affect the existence of state-level causes of conflict.

The overthrow of communism is advantageous for the cause of common security in a number of ways. Communism was the basis for the Soviet Union itself, which, combined with the Communist satellites of Central and Eastern Europe, constituted the last great multinational empire, the descendant of the empires of the French, the British, the Ottomans, the Habsburgs, and the Romanovs that once dominated the planet. The Soviet empire could remain in existence only by suppressing the forces of nationalism it harbored. Nationalist opposition to Communist rule periodically flared into open rebellion in Eastern Europe during the Cold War: in 1953 in East Germany, in 1956 in Hungary, in 1968 in Czechoslovakia, and in 1980–81 in Poland. As long as nationalist grievances persisted, which would be as long as those countries were dominated by Moscow, rebellion in different forms was bound to recur.

Such rebellions were a continuing source of conflict between the Soviet Union and the West. They reinforced the Western view that the Soviet empire itself was an act of aggression[17] and that Moscow would attempt to conquer and dominate Western Europe unless forcibly prevented from doing so. Thus the Soviet Union itself was a state-level cause of war: As long as it existed, there were limits to the confidence the West could have that Moscow's intentions toward the rest of Europe were benign.[18]

Gorbachev was committed both to the maintenance of the Soviet empire and to Soviet participation in a common security order. The two were not mutually exclusive in his mind because he believed that he could transform an empire that had been created through conquest into a voluntary commonwealth.[19] He was wrong. The dissolution of the Soviet empire made common security potentially sturdier by removing one source of the Western perception of aggressive intentions from the East.

Communism was also a continuing cause of conflict for the reason that Kennan noted in 1947: The need to maintain total control internally created the requirement for an implacable external enemy. The need for total control was part of the ideology of Marxism-Leninism, according to which it was the task of the Communist party, as the vanguard of history, to refashion society from top to bottom. That required total power: hence the term "totalitarian."

The need for absolute control stemmed as well from the origins of the Soviet state. A small group of radicals without deep roots in Russian society seized the machinery of government in the Russian capital, Petrograd, in 1917. They had narrow support in the country at the outset of their rule, which became narrower still when the radicalism of their program became apparent. Total control thus became a requirement for staying in power.

The claim of this small group to control the Russian empire rested on its official ideology, which, the Communists asserted, was based on universal and scientific truths. The Bolsheviks had the right to rule Russia, they themselves said, because they were not only riding but also driving the course of history itself. Evidence of their mastery of, and harmony with, the tides of history was the expansion of Communist rule in Europe and elsewhere. In this way, as well, communism itself was a cause of international conflict, and its disappearance an asset for the long-term prospects for common security.

The role in the actual governance of the Soviet empire of the official ideology, Marxism-Leninism, remains a matter of debate. Communist leaders after Stalin—including even Gorbachev, the best educated among them—were unfamiliar with the writings of Marx or even Lenin. Although they sometimes claimed to be latter-day versions of philosopher-kings, they were in fact bureaucratic specialists in political power. Yet the official status of the ideology, and the claims made for it, were important as the basis for whatever political legitimacy the Soviet regime possessed, and no doubt for much of the confidence with which its rulers exercised their authority. (The Soviet empire collapsed because those in power lost their confidence, which surely had something to do with the evaporation of faith in the official doctrine.)

Whatever they knew about Marx's writings, the leaders of the Soviet Union were certainly aware of one of Lenin's central beliefs: the inevitable division of the world into two irreconcilable camps that were destined to struggle for primacy across the globe. As Kennan put it in his 1947 article, "there can never be on Moscow's side any sincere assumption of a community of aims between the Soviet Union and powers which are regarded as capitalist."[20]

The Communist economic system—in which investment and production were decided by government planners on political grounds rather than by the impersonal forces of supply and demand as in the West—also contributed to features of the Soviet Union that were incompatible with common security. The Soviet Union followed what is known among economists as a pattern of "extensive" economic growth, in which increasing the gross national product depended on marshaling ever-greater quantities of "inputs": capital, labor, and raw materials. It thus differed from the Western pattern, known as "intensive growth," in which increases in national production are the result of more efficient use of constant or even decreasing quantities of these three inputs.

In the first case, direct control over territory, people, and resources is economically useful. Expansion in order to secure greater supplies of each can be economically rational. Stalin sought to exploit the territory the Red Army occupied during World War II for economic gain, stripping Eastern Europe of equipment and resources deemed economically beneficial and shipping them back to the Soviet Union.*

It is one of the insights of neoclassical economics that for a market economy formal imperial control of foreign territories does not pay. Wealth accrues from participation in the international division of labor. Thus in the eighteenth century, Great Britain did not suffer economically from the loss of the American colonies, as many British had feared it would. And thus in the twentieth century, economic efficiency and trade made Japan, poor in territory and natural resources, by some standards the richest country in the world.

The Communist economic system was also the necessary foundation of the Soviet military-industrial complex, the basis of military might that made the Soviet Union a threat to the West. The Soviet economy was sometimes called a "command" system because the regime managed it in the same way an army is run: exercising command over all the country's resources. A very large fraction of those resources was directed to military uses—as much as 30 percent of the entire Soviet output,[21] four to five times the proportion that the United States devoted to military purposes. It is perhaps less accurate to say that the Soviet Union *had* a military-industrial complex than that it *was* a military-industrial complex. The economy was operated not to promote individual welfare but rather to enhance state power.

---

*The United States took the opposite course, with better results, seeking to promote economic recovery on the territories it occupied during the course of the war by transferring resources to them through the Marshall Plan. The consequent prosperity of Western Europe made the United States itself richer and the Western military alliance it led more cohesive, legitimate, and powerful than the Communist sphere in Europe.

The command economy made it possible to sustain a global military force on a weak economic base.

The command economy depended on access to the total resources of Soviet society, and therefore required a totalitarian political system to function efficiently. The end of Communist politics thus brought to an end Communist economics; the end of Communist economics reduced the size and power of the Soviet military-industrial complex, which was further crippled by the collapse of the Soviet Union itself because key parts of it were located in places—the Baltic states and Ukraine—that escaped Moscow's control. Because Russia has a far less powerful military establishment than the Soviet Union did, and because its military *potential* is more modest, its capacity to threaten its neighbors has diminished. Thus it can fit more comfortably into the European system of common security.

The fall of communism has reinforced common security not only by reducing state-level causes of conflict but also by removing obstacles to the practices that reduce the system-level cause, the insecurity rooted in anarchy. The origins of the Communist party of the Soviet Union as a small, illegal, conspiratorial group under constant surveillance and harassment by the czarist authorities put a premium on secrecy within its ranks. The habit of secrecy persisted even when the party held sway over much of the Earth's surface. Secrecy runs counter to one of the central practices of common security: transparency. Post-Communist Russian politics have not been entirely transparent. The method by which officials in the Kremlin decided to assault Chechnya at the end of 1994 was not so different from the way their Soviet predecessors had decided to invade Afghanistan fifteen years earlier. Compared to the Soviet era, however, the procedures of government in Russia were more open.

Just as Mikhail Gorbachev did not believe that the maintenance of a Soviet empire in Europe was incompatible with common security, so he did not believe that the existence of the Soviet Union itself, under Communist rule, was necessarily incompatible with the pattern of relations with other countries that he endorsed. His life's work was to make the country he governed more open, democratic, and humane while retaining its basic political forms. Had he succeeded he would have made it more compatible with a common security order. He did not succeed in reforming the Soviet Union. Instead, it collapsed.[22] But even if he had succeeded, as long as the country's basic Communist structures remained in place, a successor would have been able to reverse what he had accomplished. Reform communism would still have been communism. With the collapse of the Soviet Union, the restoration of orthodox communism, which is radically incompatible with common security, became all but impossible.

This does not guarantee Russian fidelity to the letter or the spirit of post-Cold War international norms in Europe. It does, however, close off one avenue of retreat from them. The best assurance of Russian compliance with these norms would be the successful completion of the political project on which the country embarked after the collapse of the Soviet Union and fitfully pursued thereafter: the construction of democracy.

For there is reason to believe—all apart from the historical record—that the ideas on which democracy rests and the procedures that are central to it lend themselves to peaceful international conduct. While Communist political practices are at odds with the norms of common security, democracy is compatible with them. Specifically, democracy's distinguishing features make countries with democratic political systems more likely than others to be free of the traditional state-level causes of conflict. Democracies are also more likely to engage in political practices that help to alleviate the system-level cause of conflict: the insecurity rooted in anarchy.

Democracy does not, in the first place, readily lend itself to territorial conquest to extract wealth or impose a particular political system. Because the essence of democracy is self-government, it is a contradiction for a democratic country to govern others against their will. Historically this did not, of course, prevent democracies such as the United States, Great Britain, and France from amassing sizable empires. But the maintenance of these empires was at odds with democratic principles.

The United States and Britain coped with this contradiction by asserting, in part to persuade themselves, that their empires were temporary stewardships, that they were preparing the people they ruled—in the Philippines in the American case, in India in particular for the British—for self-government. In the end that is what they did. The contradiction between democracy and empire, moreover, was one reason that the democracies liquidated their empires in the second half of the twentieth century.

Kant and Wilson believed that democracies were not warlike because war never served the interest of the public as a whole; when the public could check the wishes of the rulers, it would therefore prevent bellicose behavior. Rousseau argued that monarchy had the same predisposition as Kennan later identified in communism, and for the same reason: It was inherently aggressive because monarchs, like Communists, were bound to seek to extend their rule externally and consolidate it internally, and war served both purposes.[23]

Aversion to war is not a universal, inevitable feature of democratic politics: Wars have often commanded broad popular support in democracies, although such conflicts have almost all been, or been portrayed as being, wars of self-defense. Public opinion has even occasionally helped to push a government into war, as in 1898 when the United States went to war with Spain. Nor have absolute rulers always sought to enhance their own power and glory through warfare. But it is undeniably more difficult for a democratically elected government like the one Woodrow Wilson headed to take a country to war than it was for the hereditary monarchs who ruled most of Europe in Kant's day or for the Communist oligarchs who presided over the Soviet Union until 1992.

Democracies are less susceptible to state-level causes of war because all have market economies.[24] This is so because for market economies, in contrast to Communist ones, market practices rather than the control of territory are the key to wealth.[25]

Moreover, the essence of a market economy is the free exchange of goods and services. Exchange takes place across, as well as within, international borders. Through trade and investment, market practices promote economic interdependence, which supplements a system of states whose supreme goal is self-protection with a community of like-minded, mutually entangled political units with a common interest in prosperity. Commerce makes foreigners less strange; it makes a country's own prosperity, if not hostage to, then at least affected by the prosperity of others. It makes war more costly. Trade is not absolute proof against war. World War I confounded the confident nineteenth-century assertion of an iron linkage between commerce and peace. But economic interdependence does bolster common security.[26]

Democratic government is, perhaps first and foremost, a set of procedures, which are compatible with common security. One procedure is central to both: transparency. Here again, democratic government is the antithesis of Communist rule. In a democracy, major decisions affecting the public, such as the structure and operation of military forces in a common security order, are visible to the entire world. Democratic transparency reinforces common security: The most important decision of all, the decision to go to war, cannot be made secretly, abruptly, or by one person. It is difficult for democracies to launch surprise attacks such as Nazi Germany's strike against Russia in 1941, Communist North Korea's assault on the south in 1950, and Iraq's invasion of Kuwait in 1990. The openness of internal political procedures, like openness in military affairs, is a confidence-building measure. If a democracy does decide to go to war, the decision will be made publicly. Even when it cannot prevent war, therefore, democracy, like common security, buys time.

Another democratic procedure lends itself to common security: the practice of resolving disputes peacefully. Democratic politics is the search for a basis for coexistence, and sometimes cooperation, with fellow citizens rather than a crusade to obliterate class enemies, as with Communist politics. Conducting internal affairs peacefully creates habits and experiences that can be transferred to international affairs. Domestic conflicts are settled by elections, not coups, which can give rise to the inclination to settle international disputes by negotiation instead of war. Insofar as the habit of conciliation extends from domestic politics to foreign policy, it contributes to common security.

The connection between democracy and peaceful international conduct is thus a matter of logic as well as of history. The generally peaceful record of relations between and among democracies is not a coincidence. There are reasons to believe that this *should* be so and that the more democratic the world becomes, the less prone to war international politics will be. Thus, while the brief, anomalous rule of a liberal Communist in the Kremlin may have been necessary to commit the Soviet Union to the norms of common security, the best chance for sustaining that commitment lies in the establishment of a working democracy in Russia.

Western policy toward post-Soviet Russia was based to a considerable extent on the assumption of a connection between democracy and peaceful international conduct. Western governments provided economic assistance to encourage the transition from a centrally planned to a market economy on the grounds that the market promotes peace, both directly through economic interdependence and indirectly by underpinning democracy, an antidote to state-level causes of conflict.

The new Russia is more democratic than the old Soviet Union, all apart from whatever effect on its political and economic evolution Western programs may have had. But it is not a firmly established democracy, nor, five years after the end of the Soviet Union, could Russia be said to be irrevocably committed to democratic procedures. The country had conducted free elections; but there was no guarantee that it would continue to hold them. The public had gained more power; but public control was not so entrenched, nor was the public's preference for peace so clear, as to engender confidence that the democratic tendency toward peaceful conduct would operate continuously in Russia.

Free speech was permitted in the new Russia as it had not been in the old Soviet Union. With the new electronic technologies of communication, moreover, it would surely not be possible for the government to control the information the Russian people received, as the Communist regime had managed to do for decades. But the heavy hand of the government in the management and dissemination of the news was still evident. While government proceedings were more transparent than in Communist days and an elected parliament carried out its deliberations publicly, much of the business of the Yeltsin presidency was conducted in secret.

Russia rejected the command economy inherited from the Soviet Union, which would have been impossible to maintain without the full complement of Communist political machinery. But the country could not immediately install a smoothly functioning market system in its place; and the kind of economic interdependence with neighboring countries that solidified the Franco-German peace after 1945 would be possible for Russia only as a result of changes in the Russian economy that could not be accomplished in a few months, or even a few years.[27]

The new Russia was not the Soviet Union; neither, however, was it a large, Slavic version of a Scandinavian country—law-abiding, tolerant, and tranquil. It was no longer Communist but not yet Western. It had experienced, indeed continued to experience, a revolution; but elements of the past persisted.[28]

The disintegration of the Soviet Union struck a powerful blow at the main pillars of the Russian international tradition, a tradition carried on by the Bolsheviks: the dominance, in international affairs, of national security objectives; a messianic ideology; ever-expanding imperial conquests; and an enormous military establishment.[29] But a tradition so recent and so much a part of the history of the country could not be fully eradicated in a matter of a few years.

Thus even a strong connection between democracy and peaceful conduct does not assure Russian compliance with the norms of common security in the short term, because in the short term Russia will not have all the features of democracy that predispose a country to these norms. Indeed, one reading of the historical record suggests that sovereign states with partially established democratic governments will be more bellicose than countries with governments that are fully and reliably either democratic or autocratic.[30]

In new democracies, political elites must suddenly compete for political support. They naturally search for issues, themes, and causes that can attract a popular following. An obvious candidate is nationalism. The strength of nationalist appeals will depend on the strength of nationalist grievances. In post-Soviet Russia such grievances are potentially powerful.

In one sense nationalism, like democracy, is incompatible with aggressive international behavior. Nationalism rests on the belief that members of the same group ought to have their own sovereign state. It is not a charter for including others. Historically, nationalism has been the great adversary of empire. But the collapse of the Soviet Union left 25 million ethnic Russians living as minorities in what had suddenly become foreign countries. Several of those countries are located precisely where Russian policy is most important for post-Cold War European security, indeed precisely where Russia intersects with the post-Cold War common security regime—to its west.

~8~

RUSSIA AND ITS NEIGHBORS

The future of the post-Cold War common security order in Europe depends on Russia: It requires the adherence of all the major powers and, of all of them, Russia is the least likely to remain committed to its norms. Commitment to common security depends not only on what kind of country Russia becomes but also on the interaction of the new Russia with its neighbors.

The new Russia, like the old Soviet Union, is a big country, so big that it inhabits three different global neighborhoods. The most important of them for the future of common security is the west, which is, in both geographic and political terms, part of the European common security order. Russia's relations with its huge eastern neighbor, China, and with the belt of former Soviet republics that are now independent states to its south, however, have the potential to affect the common security order indirectly, through their impact on Russian foreign policy to the west and on Russia itself.

If Russia defects from this new order, the defection will come in its relations with the countries to its west. Serious violations of the arms treaties to which the countries to the west are also party, or Russian infringement on the sovereign independence of its western neighbors, would reverberate westward. Hitler's decision to disregard the demilitarization provisions of the Versailles Treaty can be clearly seen in retrospect as a sign of his aggressive intentions; Russian rejection of the limits on nuclear and conventional arms embedded in the treaties signed between 1987 and 1993 would have to be interpreted in the same way.

Similarly, just as the forcible incorporation of Poland into the Soviet sphere of control after World War II triggered the Cold War by persuading the West that Moscow coveted all of Europe, so a Russian conflict with Ukraine or the Baltic states over their independence would signal a renewal of Russian imperial aspirations in Europe, and the West would respond accordingly. In 1945, what Russia did in Poland affected Germany. Half a century later what Russia does in the Baltic states and Ukraine will affect Poland, and Poland is part of the West.

Here the force of nationalism and the weight of the imperial Russian and Soviet political tradition are potentially dangerous. Because of these factors, where the Baltic states and Ukraine are concerned the rules of common security do not, in Russian eyes, necessarily apply. Those rules govern relations between and among sovereign states, but not all Russians, indeed probably only a minority, consider these and the other former Soviet republics to be fully and legitimately independent. For many Russians the end of the Soviet Union was both regrettable and reversible. In March 1996 the Russian parliament, the State Duma, passed a resolution repudiating the dissolution of the state that Lenin had assembled. The resolution had no binding force, nor did it reflect a deeply or widely held conviction of the Russian public, but it was evidence of a powerful and durable current of opinion in the ranks of the Russian political elite.

With the collapse of communism, Russia shed its centuries-old imperial identity and set about building a nation-state. But its political identity and geographic scope are not yet settled. If Russia is defined ethnically, then it spills across new international borders. Some Russians embrace such a definition. At the end of 1993, Boris Yeltsin himself pledged to protect Russians living outside the borders of the new Russian state.[1]

Russian nationalist sentiment with the potential to destroy the post-Cold War common security order comes in two varieties: One is most acutely relevant to Russia's relations with the Baltic states; the other suffuses Russia's relations with Ukraine.

Lithuania, Latvia, and Estonia were the least Soviet of the eighteen constituent republics of the Soviet Union. They were the last to be incorporated—in 1940, as a result of the Nazi-Soviet Pact of 1939. They had the closest historical, cultural, religious, and economic ties with the West. They were the republics where the sentiment for independence, the public expression of which Gorbachev's reforms made possible, came earliest and was strongest and most widespread.

Small and militarily vulnerable, they are indefensible against a determined Russian attack; but they are unlikely to be subjected to such an attack. Precisely because of their singular histories, Russians are not inclined to regard the Baltic states as a part of the historical patrimony that was wrongly taken from them at the end of 1991.

The Baltic states do have ethnic Russians within their borders, however. Their numbers are relatively small, but because the overall Baltic populations are themselves small, Russians constitute a sizable percentage of the population in each case: Half of Latvia, one-third of Estonia, and 15 percent of Lithuania are of other nationalities, in most cases Russian.

The Baltic peoples regarded the Russians in their midst as alien, unwelcome intruders, like the French *pieds noirs* in Algeria. The Russians had been brought in by an occupying power against the wishes of the local people and had never assimilated into the local culture or learned the local language. They were employed mainly in the Soviet military-industrial complex and lacked the skills to succeed in the new market economies of the independent countries in which they found themselves after the collapse of their employer, the Soviet Union.

The Balts preferred that the local Russians return to Russia, and some did. But most wished to stay. The governments of the newly independent Baltic states would have been on dubious moral and legal grounds in expelling them and, given the disparity in size and power with their giant Russian neighbor, were not in a position to try to do so against Russia's wishes. But the new governments refused to grant Russians automatic citizenship, imposing language tests and residency requirements that most could not meet. Officials of the Russian government termed these conditions human rights violations.[2] In a dispute over the status of ethnic Russians it was not beyond the realm of possibility for Moscow to try to enforce its preferences by military means.

However, the use of force was not likely. In the first place, Russia had withdrawn its troops from Baltic territory; they had been the most potent source of pressure on the Baltic governments. Secondly, the Baltic governments, in response to pressure both from Russia and Western Europe, modified their requirements, making citizenship somewhat easier, and never actively persecuted the Russians under their jurisdictions. Third, Moscow understood that the West considered the Baltic states part of Europe and that a violation of Baltic sovereignty would therefore repolarize the continent in political and perhaps military terms.

Open conflict of the kind that would subvert the post-Cold War European common security order was more likely between Russia and the largest former republic in the west. Ukraine also contained a large complement of ethnic Russians: twelve million out of a total population of fifty-two million. Many lived in the eastern part of the country, along the border with Russia, in the Donbass region, the economy of which was dominated by heavy industry and coal mines. Eastern Ukraine voted heavily for independence from the Soviet Union in December 1991, along with the rest of the country. But it was possible to imagine circumstances in which Donbass Russians would seek to leave Ukraine and join Russia, or in which Russia would seek to reassert domination over eastern Ukraine and annex it to the Russian state.

A series of specific issues divided Russia from Ukraine almost from the moment the Soviet Union disintegrated. One was the proper distribution of Soviet military assets, in particular Soviet nuclear weapons, some of which were stationed in Ukraine, and the Black Sea fleet, to which both countries laid claim.

Also in dispute was the status of the Crimean Peninsula. Inhabited largely by ethnic Russians, it had been "given" to Ukraine by the Soviet leader Nikita Khrushchev in 1954 as a symbol of the friendship and solidarity between the two peoples, to mark the 300th anniversary of what in Soviet times was celebrated as the voluntary union of Ukraine and Russia. (It was in fact the year when Cossacks in Ukraine sought protection against the Poles and Turks from the Russian czar.)

Geographically, Crimea belongs to Ukraine; it has no border with Russia. But local Russians, for ethnic, historical, and economic reasons favored remaining part of a Russian state, and many in Russia, including in the Russian parliament, supported their preference. Further complicating Crimea's status was the return from exile in Central Asia, to which Stalin had brutally consigned them in World War II, of many of the peninsula's original inhabitants, the Crimean

Tatars, a Muslim people from whose control Catherine the Great had wrested Crimea in 1783.

Economic issues also set Russia and Ukraine at odds. Russia, rich in oil and gas, was the principal source of both for Ukraine, which has none. Ukraine had difficulty paying even the artificially low price Russia initially charged, yet could not operate its economy without Russian-supplied energy. As a result, it incurred a large debt to Russia.

Still, in the first five years of the post-Soviet era the two countries managed these issues with a measure of skill, goodwill, and success. They reached agreement on the division of most Soviet military assets. Although the local parliament in Crimea was dominated by Russian secessionists who received rhetorical support in Russia itself, Moscow took no steps to assist them. Meanwhile, the two governments negotiated to reschedule Ukraine's debt.

Underlying, aggravating, and transcending these specific causes of conflict, however, and making the Russian-Ukrainian relationship more dangerous and uncertain than the sum of the bilateral disputes between the two, was the broader, more diffuse "existential" question of whether Ukraine could, and should, be an independent state.

The initial threat to its independence came from within. Ukraine experienced severe difficulty after 1991 in organizing an effective state and a viable economy. The destruction of the command system triggered by the end of Communist rule was not followed by even the slow, halting transition to a market economy that took place in Russia, but rather by hyperinflation and economic disintegration. So precarious was the Ukrainian economy in the wake of the dissolution of the Soviet Union that the collapse of the country itself seemed periodically possible.

In that case, Russia, which for all its troubles was stronger in political and economic terms, might be drawn into Ukrainian affairs regardless of whether the Russian government favored such a course. Many Russians did favor it, on the nationalist grounds that an independent Ukraine was artificial, unnatural, and temporary. Ukraine had been a part of a predominantly Russian state for so long, the languages and religions of the two peoples were so similar, and intermarriage between them had been so extensive, that many Russians could not conceive of Ukraine as a foreign country, with Kiev, by tradition the cradle of Russian civilization, a foreign capital.

For many Russians, even after the formal dissolution of the Soviet Union, the desire to reincorporate Ukraine did not qualify as an imperial ambition. For them, Ukraine was part of the Slavic core of the Russian nation and thus properly a part of the Russian state.[3]

This assumption will fade over time. A Russian generation that has grown up with Ukraine as a separate country will accept this as normal; but that will take a generation. In the short term, an independent Ukraine provides fertile ground for irredentist sentiment in Russia, which is reinforced by the misery and confusion that have followed the disintegration of the Soviet Union as well as by the fact that Ukrainian independence came without warning. The parallel with Weimar Germany is uncomfortably close. Opponents of Russian democracy have said of it what Hitler said of post-World War I German democracy: It had presided over the treacherous surrender of the country's patrimony in unholy collaboration with its Western enemies.

A Russian effort to absorb all or part of Ukraine, because of a Ukrainian collapse or as part of a concerted policy to reconstitute a greater Russian state or some combination of the two motives, would have serious consequences for Europe. It would cripple, perhaps even destroy, the post-Cold War common security order. To the extent that the reincorporation of Ukraine was successful, Russia would once again become a multinational empire with a foreign policy of expansion westward, and thus a threat to Europe.

A Russian policy of reincorporation would meet resistance in Ukraine, making both countries unstable and perhaps even triggering a full-scale war between two countries with nuclear weapons capabilities. Violent conflict between Russia and Ukraine would reverberate westward even if the fighting did not spread. All of Europe would become a more uncertain and less safe place.

During the Cold War, the inner-German border was the continent's fault line, the place where major military forces were massed and where a major war would have begun. Now the most dangerous place on the continent is the border between Russia and Ukraine. If Russian-Ukrainian relations are friendly, Russia will be seen in the West as a benevolent presence on the eastern flank of Europe. If, on the other hand, the relationship between the two becomes hostile, this will put Poland, then Germany, on alert for a revival of imperial Russian conduct. The Russian-Ukrainian bilateral relationship is therefore, in strategic terms, the single most important one in Europe.

Because there are so many similarities between them and they have so much common history, the bilateral relationship between Russia and Ukraine is an unusual one. Perhaps the closest parallels are the Canadian-American and the Indo-Pakistani relationships, both involving countries created by the violent partition of what had been a single political unit.[4] Insofar as the history of those two bilateral relationships offers clues to the future of the relationship between the two most populous successor states to the Soviet Union, the parallels are not encouraging. The optimal Russian-Ukrainian relationship is the one that the United States and Canada have maintained in the twentieth century: open borders, close economic cooperation, virtual unanimity on issues of foreign policy and security, all in the context of respect for the other's sovereignty. In the nineteenth century, however, the United States was intermittently interested in annexing Canada, an interest that persisted even after the American Civil War.

The Indo-Pakistani relationship offers an even more disquieting precedent. Since British India was divided in 1947, the two countries' relationship has been marked by hostility and suspicion punctuated by occasional wars.* After 1947, moreover, the kind of existential issue that underlies Russian-Ukrainian relations hung over the dealings between India and Pakistan. Pakistanis continually suspected that their larger neighbor did not consider their independence legitimate. At the time of partition, the leaders of the Congress party that led India to independence, Mohandas Gandhi and Jawaharlal Nehru, did oppose a separate, predominantly Muslim state, although not out of anti-Islamic prejudice but rather because they were committed to a united, secular, democratic state with full political equality for all, regardless of faith. The Pakistani elite suspected India of regarding Pakistani independence as not only undesirable but also reversible; and the Indian army did intervene militarily to enable Pakistan's eastern wing to achieve independence as Bangladesh in the 1971 Pakistani civil war.

While the historical parallels are suggestive, they are no more than that. The Russian-Ukrainian relationship is not doomed to repeat the difficulties of Canadian-American and Indo-Pakistani relations. Indeed, the early years of that relationship gave reason for encouragement. The 1994 Ukrainian presidential election brought to office Leonid Kuchma, a former factory director with strong support in the Russian-dominated eastern part of the country. Kuchma seemed more likely than the incumbent he defeated, Leonid Kravchuk, the first president of independent Ukraine, to avoid the development most dangerous for Russian-Ukrainian relations: the

---

*In the 1980s and 1990s the relationship was poisoned by an issue with a troubling similarity to the role of Crimea in Russian-Ukrainian affairs: the status of Kashmir, a Muslim-majority state acquired by India at the time of partition in a way that Pakistanis and many Kashmiris considered illegitimate. The people of Kashmir never fully accepted Indian rule and in the late 1980s mounted an insurrection against it with assistance from Pakistan.

complete collapse of the Ukrainian economy. Meanwhile, Western governments came to recognize that an independent Ukraine had a significance for the West beyond the nuclear weapons on its territory, that Ukrainian independence was in fact a Western strategic interest.

Russian-Ukrainian bilateral military relations, moreover, were governed by the principles of common security. Nuclear and non-nuclear arms in both countries were limited by treaties that formed the core of the European common security order. Each was allotted national totals of conventional armaments by the modifications made at Tashkent in 1992 to the treaty on Conventional Forces in Europe (CFE) of 1990. Nuclear weapons were covered by the April 1992 Lisbon Protocol to the 1991 START I treaty. Some of the weapons covered by that treaty, concluded when the Soviet Union was still a single state, were located in Ukraine. By the terms of the Lisbon Protocol, the Ukrainian government agreed to ship them back to Russia. When Kiev balked at carrying out this pledge, the American government stepped in to help negotiate a three-way accord involving the United States as well as Russia and Ukraine that provided a road map for doing so. As long as both countries observed the letter of these treaties, neither was likely to threaten the other and both would be part of the post-Cold War common security order.

The ultimate reabsorption of the new independent country of Belarus by Russia is more likely than the Russian annexation of Ukraine. Indeed, in March 1996 the two governments announced plans for a union of the two countries. Such a step would have implications for European security. Belarus, like Ukraine, is situated between Russia and the West. It, too, has a border with Poland. It, too, is the site of invasion routes in both directions used repeatedly over the centuries. But if the annexation were voluntary, if it were to take place without violence, if the military forces stationed in Belarus did not exceed the number it has been allotted by treaty as a sovereign state, this would not necessarily be incompatible with the perpetuation of a common security order in Europe.

Whatever the fate of Belarus, continued Russian adherence to that order cannot be taken for granted. Common security presumes the absence of state-level causes of conflict. A Russian desire to reabsorb Ukraine is such a cause. In a common security order, each country unquestioningly accepts the sovereign independence of all the others. Acceptance of the independence of its western neighbors that were once Soviet republics is far from universal in Russia. But even this, in and of itself, does not rule out Russian participation in the common security order. A belief in its precepts is the most powerful and enduring reason for a state to adhere to the norms of a common security order; but it is not the only reason.

The West, which includes the signatories to the current arms treaties from North America to Poland, is committed to common security by conviction. In Russia this conviction is weaker, both because of the fall from power of Mikhail Gorbachev, who made the initial commitment to common security norms, and for all the reasons that Russia is different from the West: a political system not yet fully and irreversibly democratic; a tradition that emphasizes authoritarian rule at home and the pursuit of empire abroad; and currents of nationalist sentiment fortified by the collapse of the Soviet Union.

Still, sovereign states, like individuals, obey rules for reasons other than the conviction that it is right to do so. Compliance without conviction is not only possible, it is common. The entire system of justice within states—police, courts, prisons—exists both to punish those who do not obey the law and to encourage obedience on the part of others. It is designed to make obedience a matter of prudence even where it is not a matter of conviction. Although there is no global government to enforce international norms and to punish those who violate them, this does not mean that such violations are necessarily cost-free. To the contrary, for Russia to adopt policies that returned the international relations of Europe to the traditional system of a balance of power would be costly, and that is the strongest reason, in the short term, to expect Russia to remain in compliance with the common security order.

Purely economic costs play a role, as demonstrated by the Russian reluctance to reintegrate Belarus.[5] The most important check on any Russian aspiration, in the wake of the Cold War to break out of the confines of the common security order, is not, however, economic prudence. It is military weakness, weakness that is only partly the consequence of treaty-imposed limits on Russian military forces.

The end of Communist rule and of the Soviet Union itself dealt a devastating blow to the basis of Soviet military might, the Soviet military-industrial complex.[6] In 1992 and thereafter, many military factories were kept functioning, often at low levels of production, by subsidies provided by Moscow through the deceptively simple technique of printing money. The Russian government waged a battle of varying intensity against the resulting inflation, periodically controlling the creation of money that went in no small part to military industries. Thus the transition to a market economy, and in particular the policies necessary for macroeconomic stability, did more to reduce the military power that communism built in Russia than all the military engagements and all the arms control accords of the Cold War.

Moreover, with the collapse of the Soviet Union, the effectiveness of the military forces that Russia continued to possess deteriorated dramatically. The manpower available to the armed forces shrunk, as young men of draft age evaded service in large numbers; in some parts of the country as few as 10 percent of those summoned to the army actually served. Funds for maintenance and training were scarce, often nonexistent. The real value of soldiers' salaries plummeted. Logistical and other support systems were disrupted. Parts of the army were reduced to "virtual self-maintenance,"[7] scavenging for food and shelter like bands of primitive hunters, often relying on local authorities rather than on the national government in Moscow.

The effect of all these changes, negotiated and unilateral, planned and unplanned, was to replace a military juggernaut stationed in the middle of Germany poised to strike west with little or no warning, with a ramshackle military force limited by treaty, subverted by the social trends that the collapse of communism had turned loose, and deployed 1,000 miles to the east of the front line of the Cold War.

This was not a military force capable of conducting effective operations on a large scale, or indeed on any scale. The war in Chechnya, which began with a Russian assault on the Chechen capital of Grozny in December 1994, was in one respect a disturbing portent. The decision to attack was made arbitrarily and secretly by President Boris Yeltsin. It demonstrated that his government was willing to use force to resolve a political dispute—albeit an internal Russian one; no foreign government recognized a Chechen right to independence—and to use it in a particularly brutal fashion.

But if the intention behind the attack on Chechnya was distressing for the future of common security, the military capabilities on display in a war that Russia started but, despite overwhelming military superiority, could not win quickly or easily, were not. The Russian war in Chechnya was fought by a ragged, demoralized, incompetent army.[8] Russia was unlikely to be able to invade neighboring countries if it could not, as in Chechnya, successfully invade itself.

International aggression was all the more unlikely because Russia's neighbors, at least the most important of them, Ukraine, were far better equipped to resist than were the Chechens. Ukraine possessed a sizable army that, while unproven in battle, was equipped with weaponry inherited from the Soviet military. At least some of that army would oppose any Russian effort to reincorporate Ukrainian territory by force.

Nor in such circumstances could Russia count on the indifference of the West. Even in a common security order, deterrence continues to operate. Russia would have to reckon with the likelihood that violating the post-Cold War order would reimpose a sharp line of division in Europe, but farther to the east than during the Cold War and with the western coalition enjoying an even greater advantage in economic and military might than was the case after 1945.

Russia had an interest in the maintenance of a common security regime to its west because of its own weakness, if for no other reason. The common security order shielded Russia from the opposition of countries that were collectively far more powerful.

Common security served another Russian purpose. Although Russians saw themselves, in the wake of communism's collapse, as the aggrieved party, the victims of an historical injustice, the new Russia would be subject for decades to its neighbors' suspicions that it aspired to repeat the foreign policy of the past. Indeed, any Russian initiative that departed from what its neighbors wanted, expected, or practiced themselves, was likely to be seen as the harbinger of aggression, a sign that the new Russia was seeking to follow the imperial path of the old one.

The common security regime has therefore made Europe safe for Russian policies beyond its borders that are different from, but not opposed to, those of the West. Common security creates a framework within which Russia can disagree with its neighbors without seeming dangerous. It makes Europe safe for an independent Russian foreign policy.

If Russian compliance with the rules of common security stems only from Russian weakness, it is unlikely to persist when Russia is no longer weak. At some point the country will regain political cohesion and economic health and thus the potential to reconstitute military power that is significant, even if not on a scale that the Soviet Union managed. The stronger Russia is, the more important conviction will become as the underpinning of a common security policy. Germany, after all, violated the demilitarization clauses of the Versailles Treaty when Hitler felt strong enough to do so.

Here, once again, time can work in favor of common security norms. Like confidence-building measures, Russian weakness provides warning time for Russia's neighbors. There is a long road, and many intermediate steps, between the Russia of the mid-1990s and a Russia that could threaten Europe in anything approaching the way the Soviet Union did. If Russia should set out on that road the West would have considerable advance notice. There would be time to recognize the return of the old Russia and to respond to the dangers it would pose.[9]

Moreover, in the time required for Russia to make the transition from weakness to strength, conviction could take root, if only through familiarity and the force of habit. The longer Russia lives within the constraints of common security, the more fully its military forces are structured to comply with the arms treaties at the core of the common security order, and to the extent that the Russian military industry is rebuilt to sustain those and not other forces, what was unthinkable during the Soviet era, and in the early years of the post-Soviet period was seen as alien and obnoxious, could come to seem normal: a Russia at peace with independent neighbors and a Russian military capable of defending Russia's borders but not of expanding them.

Necessity, the basis for Russian adherence to the common security order in the immediate aftermath of the Cold War, could ultimately become the mother of legitimacy. Nations, like individuals, can begin by doing things because they have to and end by doing them because they want to, or because they cannot imagine not doing them. For Russia, the common security order at the outset of the post-Soviet era was a shoe that pinched. Over time it might, like well-worn shoes, become so comfortable that the Russian government and public would not notice it.

Even the transformation of the basis of compliance from necessity to conviction, however, would not guarantee Russian participation in the European common security order. Foreign policy, like other kinds of behavior, is shaped by the surrounding environment. Russia's neighborhood to the west is benign, but it is not the only neighborhood in which the new Russia must live. With its neighbors to the east and south, the dependably peaceful relationship with the west will not necessarily be possible. Russia may conduct a foreign policy to the east that departs sharply from the practices of common security in Europe. It has already done so to the south. In the worst case, policies it adopted in one or both of those other two neighborhoods could spill over to Russia's relations to the west.

Just as the West's relations with Russia depend partly on what happens within Russia, so Russia's relations with China depend on internal Chinese developments. As with Russia, China's fate is uncertain, and for the same reasons. Both are politically and economically in transition, and, in a sense, in limbo: no longer orthodox Communist countries but not well-established democracies either. Like Russia, China has no history as a democracy. Like Russia, China is large enough to resist the pull of the prevailing political and economic trends in its region. As with Russia, nothing in the Chinese tradition provides a basis for interacting with neighboring countries according to the principles of common security. Nor do recent relations between Russia and China suggest common security as the most likely basis for their relations in the future. Although not perennial adversaries, in the view of many Chinese, the czars took advantage of China's nineteenth-century weakness to seize territory that was rightfully Chinese.[10] Sino-Soviet relations after Mao Zedong's Communists took power in 1949 were plagued by suspicion and testiness, flaring into open warfare on a small scale in 1969.[11] For the next two decades an armed truce prevailed, a Sino-Soviet equivalent of the Cold War to the west.

The Soviet Union's relations with China, as with the West, were transformed by Mikhail Gorbachev. The Chinese government had insisted that Moscow take three steps to improve Sino-Soviet relations: reduce Soviet troops on the Chinese border; withdraw Soviet forces from Afghanistan; and end Soviet support for the Vietnamese-sponsored government of Cambodia. Gorbachev gave China satisfaction on all three, paving the way for his trip to Beijing in May 1989. That visit was overshadowed by the pro-democracy demonstrations in Beijing and elsewhere that ended with the army firing on demonstrators in Tiananmen Square in the heart of the Chinese capital.

When the Soviet Union collapsed, Chinese leaders reacted with a mixture of relief at the weakening of a powerful neighbor, dismay at the rejection of an ideology the Chinese version of which justified their own rule, and ultimately satisfaction at the chaos into which the new Russia seemed to fall. Russia's fate after communism was, Chinese leaders believed, a powerful argument in favor of perpetuating Communist rule in their own country so as to spare China the same fate.

China's border with the new Russia was shorter than the one it had had with the Soviet Union. Part of the old border now divides China from three newly independent Central Asian countries: Kazakhstan, Kyrgyzstan, and Tajikistan. Official Sino-Russian relations after the end of the Soviet Union were generally distant and wary—neither cordial nor hostile, although an April 1996 visit to Beijing by Boris Yeltsin reflected a joint desire to make them warmer.

There was reason to expect this state of affairs to continue. The priority of China's government, as for the last Communist government of the Soviet Union, was domestic rather than foreign affairs, and above all the promotion of economic growth.

International conflict involving China, moreover, was more likely to take place to its east and south—over what it regarded as unwarranted American intrusion into its internal affairs on behalf of human rights, over Beijing's claim to islands in the Spratly chain in the South China Sea, and over the Communist regime's insistence that Taiwan was a Chinese province. The escalation to violent conflict of any of these three issues had the potential to trigger a wider war, involving the United States. In none of the three, however, would China confront Russia.

Still, Sino-Soviet relations did have the potential to deteriorate. The population imbalance in the border regions was a potential cause of friction; in the last years of the Soviet Union, Chinese began to cross the border in increasing numbers, most to trade but some to stay and work.[12] Russians began to fear that the far more numerous Chinese in the region would launch a creeping, informal colonization of Russian territory.

Islamic peoples in China's west grew restive in the first half of the 1990s, inspired by the independence won by members of their ethnic groups and coreligionists in Central Asia. Open conflict between them and the Chinese government in Beijing had the potential to draw in their neighbor Russia as their protector.

Beyond any specific differences, Sino-Russian relations were likely to be marked by the general suspicion that two large nations with no history of friendship or cooperation, each prone to outbreaks of xenophobia, sharing a long border and armed with nuclear weapons, are bound to have for each other.[13] This unavoidable mutual wariness would be compounded, on the Russian side at least, by the abrupt

reversal of what had been the familiar roles of the two countries in the modern period. China was now rising sharply in
power, wealth, and prestige, while Russia was, by the same
criteria, in sharp decline. Sino-Russian relations could thus
revert to the old familiar pattern of balance of power.

Sino-Russian relations bear on the post-Cold War
common security order insofar as they affect Russian policy toward Europe. A Russian balance of power policy to
the east could spill over to the west: Russia is, after all, one
country, with a single set of institutions, a single leadership,
and a single military establishment, which might not wish
or be able to divide its foreign policy toward the west from
its policy to the east.

The logic of balance of power politics, however, suggests the opposite outcome. According to this logic, in the
interest of self-protection, Russia would be likely to sustain
peaceful ties to the west, the better to concentrate its military
resources on its eastern flank.[14] Far from eroding the Russian
commitment to common security, adversarial relations with
China, like Russia's military weakness, might fortify it, for
reasons of prudence.

To the south, Russia pursued neither common security
nor a balance of power. Relations with the new, weak, and
unstable countries of the Caucasus and Central Asia that
had once been Soviet republics could fairly be described as
"neoimperialist." Russia's government proclaimed the
entire territory of the former Soviet Union to be a sphere of
special Russian responsibility. Russia's ultimate aim there,
according to one official, was the creation of "a single army,
a single border system, a single economic space."[15] The combination of statements, aspirations, and predictions about
Russian primacy came to be known as the Russian version
of the American Monroe Doctrine.[16]

Five years after the collapse of the Soviet Union, Russia
had neither fully reintegrated Belarus nor acquired a special
role in the internal affairs of the Baltic states or Ukraine. To

the south, by contrast, Moscow was deeply involved in the internal affairs of the successor states to the Soviet Union.

The newly independent states of the south were the sites of Russian military bases. Russian personnel patrolled their southern borders, which Moscow deemed the de facto southern borders of Russia. Bilateral treaties of military cooperation were signed, and there was discussion of a NATO-style integrated military organization.[17] Local armies were staffed with ethnic Russian officers, and the command structures, equipment, and military doctrines were Russian.[18] Russia was deeply engaged, either as a mediator or as an ally of one of the belligerents, in several of the conflicts that raged to its south: between Armenia and Azerbaijan over Nagorno-Karabakh, for instance, and in the civil wars in Georgia and Tajikistan. All told, some 130,000 Russian troops were deployed south of Russia's new borders.[19] In some cases Russia intervened after the end of the Soviet Union; in others, it never left.

Russia's post-Soviet role to its south partly continued the political, economic, and military patterns of the Soviet Union. Moscow did not treat its southern neighbors as fully sovereign.[20] But what Russia did also broke with the patterns of the Soviet era. The Russian Monroe Doctrine did not replicate the Brezhnev Doctrine, which asserted the right of the Soviet Union to maintain Communist governments in power by whatever means necessary. Russia made no effort to reimpose communism, or impose any other form of government. Nor did Moscow formally challenge the sovereignty achieved by the formerly Soviet republics of the Caucasus and Central Asia after 1991.[21]

The Russian role was neither uniformly intrusive everywhere to the south nor the product of a grand design. In no place did it stem from a drive to expand based on a messianic ideology of the kind that had fueled the czarist and Communist conquests.

In some cases—in Tajikistan, for example—Russia was drawn in by its concern that local instability, if unchecked, would spread northward. Like other countries, Russia was uncomfortable with turmoil on its borders, which it tried to pacify by inserting its forces. "If we do not . . . conduct peacekeeping missions in the zone of the former Soviet Union," Foreign Minister Andrei Kozyrev said in a September 1993 speech at the United Nations, "this vacuum will be filled by other forces, first of all by the forces of political extremism, which, ultimately, threaten Russia herself."[22] Traditional geopolitical motives also came into play. Moscow was wary of the growth of Turkish and Iranian influence, particularly in the Caucasus.

In several of the Central Asian states a Russian presence was welcomed by local leaders, who saw it as a way to bolster their own personal authority.[23] Over the long term, perhaps the most important and enduring motive for Russian engagement to the south was energy. The Russian government sought a share of the wealth that the vast energy deposits in the Caspian Sea basin and in Central Asia would generate. It thus sought a measure of control over the pipelines built to carry the oil and natural gas to the West in exchange for hard currency. Because the energy supplies and the revenues at stake were enormous, Russian interest in the region was likely to be substantial and enduring.

Aside from securing some benefit from the energy deposits there, however, the Russian motives for entanglement to the south were largely defensive. Defensive motives—stopping trouble at a distance before it advances closer to home—can underwrite the expansion of imperial control on a very large scale.[24] But these motives differed from those bearing on Moscow's relations with its new neighbors to the west. There the incentives for expansion were in some ways stronger, having to do with identity rather than prosperity, involving Russia's own definition of the Russian nation and the territorial limits of the Russian state.

What drew Russia into the south—instability and energy—was thus not necessarily relevant for its policies

to its west. If Russia were to implement to its west the policies that it was carrying out in the south, this would seriously damage, if not shatter, the common security order.
But what happened to the south would not necessarily spill
over to the west. The Soviet invasion of Afghanistan in
December 1979 galvanized a vigorous Western response
because it bespoke aggressive intentions worldwide.
Russian intervention in Tajikistan does not have the same
significance.

Russia's role to the south did threaten the common
security order directly in one way, however. The Russian
government insisted on modifying one of the subtotals of
the CFE treaty, the "southern flank" limits, so that it could
legally deploy more forces in southern Russia. Its purpose
was to pacify Chechnya and project influence into the
Caucasus. Russian forces were not in compliance with that
part of the treaty when it officially went into effect in
November 1995. The limits were originally negotiated at
the behest of Turkey, an historic adversary of Russia and a
member of NATO.

The forces that Russia retained to the south did not
overturn the CFE treaty or the common security order as a
whole. They did not pose a military threat to Turkey. The
violation was a technical one; but it was a violation nonetheless and thus a troubling development because a bad precedent, casting doubt on Russia's commitment to the full
range of its treaty obligations.[25]

The Russian role to the south posed a potential threat to
common security in the west in an indirect way as well. In
Russian history, expansion abroad went hand in hand with
autocracy at home. The Russian state was designed for conquest. In the Soviet period, economic and political structures were organized to maximize military power. What
makes democracy the optimal form of government for common security also makes it disadvantageous for the accu-
mulation of military power, war, and conquest.

Russian imperialism to the south, therefore, was at best unlikely to reinforce democracy at home. To the extent that Russia faltered in the pursuit of democracy at home, it would likely be less committed to the norms of common security to the west. Such a chain of cause and effect, however, was not inevitable.

Western nations acquired and governed imperial possessions abroad while remaining democratic, in fact while becoming more democratic, at home. In nineteenth-century Britain, the empire and the franchise expanded simultaneously. While the Western examples do not prove that Russian policies in the Caucasus and Central Asia will not corrupt or even subvert Russia's fragile democratic structures, they do demonstrate that it is not impossible for democracy and imperialism to coexist.

To summarize: In the network of treaties, policies, and attitudes that comprise the post-Cold War common security order in Europe, Russia is the weak link. Because Russia's future is uncertain, so too is its adherence to the norms of common security, which makes the future of the common security order itself uncertain. It is all too easy to imagine how and why Russia would defect from that order. But it is not a certainty that this will come to pass.

The best assurance of compliance with common security norms is democratic government. Russia may not become a full-fledged Western-style democracy, at least not soon. But even if it does not, it will not necessarily abandon the treaty commitments that it has made; prudential reasons to observe them, based on its own weakness, will remain.

Russia's relations with China could become rocky, as they were during much of the Cold War. Moscow could revert to a military standoff with, and a balance of power policy toward, China. Even in that event, however, Russia would not necessarily abandon common security policies to the west. Russian policies to the south are more predictable. For years, if not decades, they will, in some ways, resemble imperial behavior. While such policies will not bolster the commitment to common security to the West, neither will they necessarily doom it.

Russia is the weak link, but not necessarily a fatally weak one. The case for believing that the common security order can be sustained is at least as strong as the case to the contrary. The West can have only modest influence over the features of Russian political life that will determine its approach to the common security order. To encourage the maintenance of that order on Europe's eastern flank, the most important thing the West can do is to sustain its western flank. That depends on something that is, in the post-Cold War era, widely presumed but not fully assured: the continuing engagement in Europe's security affairs of the other non-European power that had dominated Europe militarily during the Cold War—the United States.

~9~

THE UNITED STATES AND EUROPE

In 1826 the British foreign minister George Canning declared that he had "called the New World into existence to redress the imbalance of the Old."[1] He was referring to London's recognition of Latin American independence, with the potential gains that could follow in Europe for Great Britain. In the twentieth century the phrase took on a different meaning. Three times the United States intervened militarily in Europe to prevent a single European power from dominating the continent: imperial Germany in World War I, Nazi Germany in World War II, and the Soviet Union in the Cold War. Canning's phrase in this sense, therefore, captures one of the main themes of the international relations of Europe in the twentieth century.

It has also been *the* main theme of American foreign policy in this century. All of philosophy, the English philosopher Alfred North Whitehead once wrote, is a series of

155

footnotes to Plato. Of American foreign policy during the Cold War it might similarly be said that it was a series of footnotes to NATO. The leadership of the Atlantic Alliance was the first and most important international commitment of the United States. Europe was the site of the largest overseas contingent of American troops. It was the basis for the nation's military planning: American armed forces were structured to fight a major war on the European continent.

The United States had political interests and military commitments all over the world, fighting two major wars in Asia. The wars, interests, and commitments outside Europe, however, all stemmed from and were seen as part of the conflict with the Soviet Union. That conflict's point of origin and center of gravity was Europe. The United States became a global power after 1945 as a consequence of the status it assumed as a peacetime European power.

While the end of the Cold War and the collapse of the Soviet Union eliminated the original reason for American intervention in Europe, the European demand for an American role in the military affairs of the continent has persisted. All four futures for European security discussed in the preceding chapters—the continuation of the status quo, out-of-area missions for NATO, the expansion of the Atlantic Alliance to include Central Europe, and a common security order—assume that the United States will remain a European power.

The status quo is attractive precisely because of the American role in it. In Bosnia, the prototypical out-of-area mission, the United States played a leading part, conducting aerial bombardment of the Bosnian Serbs, mediating among the warring parties to achieve a settlement in Dayton, Ohio, and contributing 20,000 troops to the 60,000-person military force sent to Bosnia to implement it.

NATO expansion also presumes a leading American role. The Western Europeans want the United States to share the costs; the Eastern Europeans want the United States to share the risks. Indeed, for the Eastern Europeans the value of NATO membership lies in the American commitment that comes with it. They are not confident that Western Europe could shield them from a resurgent Russia. Nor would they be entirely comfortable without a friendly country to counterbalance Germany. Although they are on good terms with their nearest and most powerful Western European neighbor in the wake of the Cold War, this has not always been true.

As for the best of the four options for European security—common security—it, too, is compatible with the continuing engagement of the United States in European affairs through the Atlantic Alliance. The persistence of NATO meets the legal requirements of the common security regime: The United States was party to treaties comprising its core and was allocated quotas of military forces along with the other signatories. Indeed, the United States is a necessary part of common security: It possesses most of the Western allotment of nuclear weapons. The withdrawal of its nuclear umbrella from Europe would put pressure on Germany to undertake its own nuclear protection, which would call into question the security policies of all the rest of Europe.

One of the advantages of common security is that it neither excludes nor alienates Russia. The perpetuation of NATO with the United States in a leading role is consistent with the consensual spirit of common security. However strongly they opposed its expansion, Russians did not necessarily oppose its survival.[2]

An American role in Europe is desirable from the European perspective because of the size and strength of the United States and the distance between North America and Europe. The United States has been a peaceful, dependable, and disinterested presence in Europe, with no wish to exercise dominion over the continent. Just what role in Europe the United States would play would ultimately be decided by the American people. In the wake of the Cold War, their continued support for such a role—normal, natural, indeed inevitable though the history of the twentieth century had made it seem—was not assured.

It was geography that cast doubt on the American role in European affairs. What made an American presence acceptable to Europe—the distance from the continent of the United States—also made that presence difficult to assure. Because it is separated from Europe by the Atlantic Ocean, the United States became part of European affairs by dint of policy rather than geography; and policy can change.

While an American presence in Europe was normal in the second half of this century, it is not inevitable in the next one. The same conditions that render common security possible—the absence of great-power conflict in Europe—make the Cold War role of the United States seem unnecessary.

As that conflict subsided, the United States began to demobilize. The American defense budget, the number of American military personnel on active duty, and the complement of American troops stationed in Europe all declined after 1989. Because defense spending remained high by most standards, however,[3] if the absence of an adversary made it seem unnecessary, the cost of the American presence in Europe was likely to make it increasingly unpopular with the American public.

Even at the height of the Cold War, the American military mission in Europe was not unreservedly popular. What was unpopular was not the commitment to Europe itself but rather the American share of the overall cost of Western defense. The Americans regularly insisted that the Europeans bear more of the burden of defending themselves.

In the post-Cold War era the resentment of the American public might become focused not on paying too much to defend Europe but rather on paying anything at all. The nations of Europe are among the wealthiest on Earth: The countries of the European Union number 375 million people and have a total annual economic output of about $7.5 tril-lion.[4] Americans may conclude that there is no reason that the Europeans should not bear the entire burden of defend-ing themselves, especially because that burden, in the wake of the Cold War, is historically light. With a central issue in post-Cold War American political life being how, and how much, to reduce government expenditures, it would be all too easy for NATO to be viewed as yet another example of a government program that has outlived its usefulness, a sub-sidy for a constituency that is politically influential rather than objectively worthy. Europe could come to appear to Americans to be a large, wealthy, undeserving welfare case, indeed one whose own vitality has been sapped by its dependence on American protection.[5]

An American retreat from Europe is possible, finally, because it was the settled policy of the United States before the Cold War to avoid engagement in the politics of the con-tinent in peacetime, and prior to World War I to avoid entan-glement in European political affairs at any time. For most of its history the United States was, by political conviction as well as geography, emphatically not a European power.

The proper meaning of "isolationism," a central precept of American foreign policy from the presidency of George Washington to that of Woodrow Wilson, is not the avoid-ance of all contact with any other country, which was impossible even in the eighteenth century and is a condition to which the American republic never aspired. Isolationism refers, rather, to the ingrained habit of steering clear as far as possible of the rivalries of the European great powers because immersion in them was corrupting and dangerous and sacrificed the benefits of one of the country's great strategic assets: the Atlantic Ocean. Isolation—it is perhaps better to call it aloofness from Europe—is an old American tradition, the two bases for which have endured: geogra-phy and the sense that the United States is and ought to remain different from Europe.[6]

It is not, however, a recent tradition. Moreover, it is a tradition that, like its opposite, the commitment to Europe of the last half century, was created and sustained under particular circumstances, few of which have survived. By the end of the Cold War, an American presence in Europe was no longer a break with tradition; it was itself traditional. In the mid-1990s, scarcely any adult American knew a world in which isolationism was even conceivable, let alone respectable. Americans had become accustomed to a security role in Europe, a role associated both with the long peace of the Cold War and the triumphs of 1989 and 1991.

Nor did a European presence corrupt the republican institutions and practices of the United States, as the founders of the American republic had feared. Their fear had rested on the conviction that the political affairs of Europe were dominated by war and the constant readiness to wage it, which was bound to subvert the republican principles on which the new American republic was founded. The large military establishment that constant readiness for war required would, they believed, threaten the limited government and even the civilian rule that were the essence of eighteenth-century republicanism.

The United States did not become less democratic in the second half of the twentieth century; if anything, the opposite was the case. Entanglement in European affairs produced no military coup, no sharp or lasting erosion of civil liberties. The power of the presidency increased, but that had happened during wartime throughout American history.

Although the original purpose of the American presence in Europe is gone, a compelling reason for sustaining a presence of some kind remains. Deterrence may no longer be necessary but reassurance serves the national interest of the United States. All the European governments want the Americans to stay. An American presence, although not cost-free, would certainly be less expensive than during the Cold War. There is reason to believe that this is an expense that the American taxpayers will be willing to bear.

In the wake of the Cold War, the United States will certainly not give up all of its armed forces. Increasingly, it is likely to provide nuclear protection (or nuclear reassurance), intelligence, military transportation and communications equipment, and technically sophisticated weapons. These are things that only the United States can produce and would be likely to produce even without a commitment to Europe, in order to remain, in some important categories, the world's leading military power. Under this scenario, the responsibility for fielding ground troops, the most expensive and politically controversial element of Western defenses, would increasingly rest with the Europeans.

American forces that are mobile or, as in the case of aircraft and nuclear weapons, of long range, or both, could continue to be designated for Europe. Given the history of American involvement in Europe in the twentieth century, they are likely to be seen by others as part of the military balance on the continent.* It would require strenuous effort to persuade the world that the United States would not involve itself in European affairs.

---

* During the Cold War, American officials sought to assure allies and adversaries that the United States was committed to the defense of Western Europe, to persuade the world that the two were "coupled" like separate cars on a single railroad train. Demonstrating the existence of coupling was considered difficult, or at least something requiring deliberate effort. In the post-Cold War world it may be that, in the minds of would-be European aggressors, it is decoupling that will seem implausible, even if the American government should try to achieve it. During the Cold War it was suggested that nuclear weapons gave rise to "existential deterrence" in that they were so potent and destructive that they gave immunity from direct attack to their possessors whatever the expressed doctrine governing their use. Similarly, the history of American foreign policy in the twentieth century may have created, in the minds of others, an "existential coupling" between the United States and Western Europe.

Still, the perceived connection will depend in part on the announced intentions of the American government, and even more on the military forces the United States actually deploys. Both will depend, in turn, on the wishes of the American public. In all democracies, especially the United States, public opinion is sovereign, and it is thus on public opinion that the future of the American role in Europe depends. The instrument for measuring public opinion is the poll. The evidence provided by polls is not an entirely reliable guide to what the country believes on any given subject, not because polls are inaccurate but because opinion is unstable. Opinions change suddenly, as well as over time, and on a range of subjects are weakly held or not held at all. The answers polls elicit depend heavily on the phrasing of the questions they pose: A change of wording can alter the result on almost any given issue.

Opinion on foreign policy issues tends to be less firmly fixed than on domestic matters because it is the product of indirect experience. Americans base their views on the state of the American economy, for example, on the income they receive and the prices they pay. They must base what they think about Bosnia, Russia, and Mexico on information that comes to them at second hand, mediated by others, through what they read in newspapers, hear on the radio, or see on television. Dramatic events can alter public opinion on foreign policy suddenly and substantially because they can change the public's picture of the world in a way that is rare for domestic issues.

Foreign policy public opinion is even less clearly defined in the post-Cold War era than earlier because of the absence of the framework, consisting of a set of stable assumptions and familiar categories, that the conflict with the Soviet Union provided. For all these reasons, surveys of American opinion on foreign policy in general and of opinion on the American role in Europe in particular provide at best a hazy, fluid picture of one of the crucial building blocks of the common security order.

Nonetheless, from these surveys some general points can be deduced.[7] First, in the post-Cold War era, no substitute for the Cold War has appeared. The conflict with the Soviet Union was the focal point, the lodestar, for the public's picture of the world and of the proper American role in it. It has not been replaced.

Second, foreign policy has had less salience in the 1990s than during the Cold War.[8] This is not surprising. People tend to be concerned about what directly affects them. War is the single most affecting international event, and the war with communism is over. In its wake, Americans have worried more about economic than about military competition.[9] On a list of important issues facing the country those involving foreign policy have, since the end of the Cold war, consistently ranked at the bottom.

Still, isolationist sentiment has not risen markedly. To the question of whether the United States should withdraw from world affairs, the affirmative response was consistently low.[10] Majorities still favored participation in NATO.[11] While giving no clear indication of precisely what kind of foreign policy can command public support in the United States, this does at least demonstrate that in the post-Cold War era the American public neither wants nor expects the absence of any foreign policy.

If there is no demand for withdrawal from the world, however, neither is there evidence of support for increasing the national attention and resources devoted to the world beyond America's borders. No constituency has emerged for restoring the place foreign policy occupied in national affairs for the half-century between the attack on Pearl Harbor and the collapse of the Soviet Union.[12]

There is thus support in the United States for some American role in Europe, but not necessarily for a role of Cold War dimensions. A majority of the American public favors continuing American participation in NATO without designating what kind of NATO it favors. Whether the public will sustain an American presence in Europe over the long term will depend on the character, the purpose, and the cost of that presence. Some of the futures for the alliance are more likely than others to command support.

The four discussed in the preceding pages can be divided, for this purpose, into two groups: the first, which includes out-of-area missions for the Atlantic Alliance and NATO expansion, is more expensive than the second—the status quo and common security.

The support the two expensive futures have enjoyed among the American public has been tentative and fragile. The circumstances in which NATO dispatched a peace-keeping force to Bosnia—only after the fighting had stopped, for a period of time too brief to assure any stable political result, and against the wishes of a majority of the American people—do not suggest a solid base of public support for this particular mission, let alone for similar operations in the future.

As for NATO expansion, the member governments' commitment to this step barely registered with their publics. When asked, 42 percent of American respondents said they favored the measure. But the respondents were not asked to consider the costs or risks involved. In the same survey, only 32 percent of Americans said they were willing to defend Poland if it were attacked by Russia, a step that an expanded NATO would be required to take.[13] The question was sufficiently remote from the immediate concerns of all but the most devoted professional students and practitioners of foreign policy that the answers, even in a sophisticated, reliable survey, were not a good indicator of anything. At the least, they revealed no large, solid, mass constituency in the United States for expanded NATO membership.

Robust and widespread public support for the two most ambitious adaptations of the Atlantic Alliance to the post-Cold War world was thus, five years after the end of the Soviet Union, not detectable. But neither adaptation was necessary to perform the central task of a European security order: to prevent a great war of the kind that was fought twice in the twentieth century.

Both were unnecessary because of the absence, in the wake of the Cold War, of great-power rivalries in Europe. The war in Bosnia did not trigger World War III because there was no one to fight it. Expanding NATO was not needed to defend the territorial integrity of the Visegrad countries because in the mid-1990s this was not in jeopardy. Both the limited risks to the peace of Europe that the fighting in Bosnia posed and the freedom from the danger of aggression enjoyed by the countries of Central and Eastern Europe had a common cause: Russian weakness.

Some of the proponents of expansion argued that Russia would not always be weak and that when it became strong it would not be benign. They further argued that waiting to extend the alliance's protection to Central and Eastern Europe until a genuine threat materialized would be dangerous. In that case, they feared, the Western powers would seek to avoid conflict with Russia, just as they had with Germany between the two world wars, leading to dire consequences. At the outset of Hitler's campaign to overturn the post-World War I settlement, Germany was weak enough to be stopped with relative ease; but the democracies acquiesced in what he did. When they did recognize the threat that his policies posed, they shrank from resistance because the cost of doing so had risen. When resistance could no longer be avoided, stopping Germany cost millions of lives.

Yet the United States behaved differently during the Cold War, mobilizing on a number of occasions to meet perceived increases in the threat posed by the Soviet Union. In 1947, in response to the political weakness of Western Europe, the United States issued the Truman Doctrine and established the Marshall Plan. In 1950, Washington intervened on the Korean Peninsula to prevent the Communist North from conquering the South. The American government twice increased defense spending sharply during peacetime, after the Soviet launch of the first Earth-orbiting satellite, Sputnik, in 1958 and after the Soviet invasion of Afghanistan in 1979.[14] The postwar record does not suggest that the American public would shrink from responding vigorously to the rise of a Russian threat to Europe: Americans were neither feeble nor timorous after 1945; to the contrary, they were resolute.

The American role in the other two futures for European security—the status quo and common security—would be far less taxing. In fact, the requirements of the two are the same: an American commitment to Europe in some form, although not necessarily in the same form and certainly not at the same force levels of the Cold War. Further, in neither case is the American military presence directed against a specific adversary. In both cases it is designed to prevent a spiral of mistrust from developing. The rationale is the same in both cases: to reassure the countries of Europe that the distribution of military power among them will not change suddenly or dramatically.

In both the NATO status quo and the post-Cold War common security order, the American commitment to Europe reassures Germany that it will not have to safeguard its own security by itself, a task that would make the acquisition of a more powerful military force, including nuclear weapons, seem tempting, perhaps even necessary to the Germans. The belief that German security policy will not change reassures Germany's neighbors, including Russia.

At the same time, the American presence reassures other countries about Russia, giving them reason to feel confident that if Europe should once again be threatened by an imperial Russian foreign policy, the United States would stand ready to organize and fortify an opposing coalition. Where Russia and Germany, the two potential revisionist powers, are concerned, an American commitment to Europe offers the benefits of containment without its drawbacks. The American presence stands as a barrier against a campaign of territorial aggrandizement by either while at the same time being acceptable to both. The American presence in Europe is, in short, a confidence-building measure.

Precisely what American military presence the two less taxing futures require is not easy to stipulate. To the perennial military question "how much is enough?" for the mission of reassurance the answer is particularly hard to fix because it is a psychological more than a military undertaking. But here, again, the passage of time is relevant.

Over time, all Europeans can gain confidence in the stability of the post-Cold War arrangements, in which case the size of the American force necessary to shore up that confidence would diminish. The more confidence there is, over time, the fewer American troops will be needed.

Five years after the collapse of the Soviet Union, there were relatively few American nuclear weapons on European soil, suggesting that the requirement for making the American nuclear guarantee credible had become, in German eyes, more modest. The Clinton administration pledged that the number of American troops stationed in Europe would not fall below 100,000; but even if it should do so, even if one day there should be no troops at all, this would not necessarily be incompatible with the maintenance of the basic political structure of the Atlantic Alliance or with the common security order.

In that case, the American role in Europe would revert to what the post-World War II founders of the alliance had envisioned. When the North Atlantic Treaty was signed in 1949, a permanent American garrison on the continent was not contemplated. To the contrary, the Truman administration assured the Congress that nothing of the sort was anticipated.[15] It was only in 1950, when the outbreak of the Korean War turned the Cold War, in American eyes, from a political and economic competition with communism into a military challenge from the Soviet Union and its allies, that NATO was transformed from a guarantee pact to an integrated military force. In its original conception, the Atlantic Alliance was simply a promise by the United States to come to Europe's rescue for a third time in the twentieth century if necessary. There is no threat of direct attack against the West in Europe because there is no army capable of mounting one. Thus, the American role as originally conceived may once again become adequate to assure the goal of the treaty: peace and stability on the continent.

In these circumstances, the American military presence is like a brace on the leg of a basketball player who once needed it to protect an injured knee but who continues to wear it, out of force of habit or superstition or subconscious need, or a combination of all three, long after the injury has fully healed. Because a knee brace is considerably less expensive to maintain than several modern, well-equipped divisions of American troops, a different medical metaphor may be appropriate for the future of the American military presence in Europe. Surgical stitches are now made of organic material and do not have to be removed; they simply dissolve as the wound heals. Similarly, the American military presence might, over time, if all goes well in Europe and common security takes firm root, slowly, quietly, and imperceptibly fade away.

Whatever American military presence the two mutually compatible and in some ways identical futures for European security—the status quo and common security—require, it is likely to be more readily supported by the American public than an out-of-area vocation for, or an expanded version of, the Atlantic Alliance. The less expensive of the four are more compatible with the ongoing demobilization of American military forces and with the widely held sense that, with the end of the Cold War, the world has become a less dangerous place demanding less strenuous exertions from the United States. While public opinion may not permit the United States to do as much as it did in Europe during the Cold War, the changes in Europe that the end of the Cold War has brought make it unnecessary for the West's strongest power to do as much as it did. What is less burdensome economically and more feasible politically is also more desirable strategically.

For domestic reasons the United States will have to have a more modest military presence in Europe; but for strategic reasons it can afford to have a more modest presence. Indeed, as long as Russia abides by the norms of common security, the United States should maintain a more modest presence. In the case of the American role in Europe at the outset of the post-Cold War era, for once all good things do go together.

CONCLUSION

*I*n January 1991, President George Bush proclaimed that the American-led effort to drive Saddam Hussein's army from Kuwait heralded the dawn of "a new world order where diverse nations are drawn together in common cause to achieve the universal aspirations of mankind—peace and security, freedom, and the rule of law."[1]

It proved to be a false dawn. The world became less rather than more orderly in the wake of the Cold War, but outbreaks of instability beyond the Middle East did not attract the attention that Iraq's occupation of Kuwait received. The powerful multinational firefighting squad that put out the blaze in the Persian Gulf proved to be unavailable elsewhere. There was, and is, no new world order of the kind that Bush foresaw.

There was, and is, however, a new security order in Europe. To be sure, it does not abolish all organized violence there. It neither prevented nor quickly stopped the fighting in the former Yugoslavia. But it does reduce to historically low levels the chances of a major war, involving all the major powers, like the two world wars of the twentieth century. The establishment of that order represents the dawn of peace in Europe.

The new common security order is the product of the interaction of three great changes in Europe in the late 1980s and early 1990s. One is a change in the political map of the continent. The collapse of the Soviet empire in Central Europe liberated nominally independent sovereign states that had been under Moscow's effective control; the collapse of the Soviet Union itself led to the independence, in most cases for the first time in modern history, of countries that had been republics–provinces–of the Soviet Union.

The dissolution of the last great multinational empire on the planet eliminated a standing cause of war in Europe. The nations that Moscow dominated were perpetually willing, although only occasionally able, to rise up against Communist rule. The control that Moscow exercised was regarded in the West, as well as in the Soviet-dominated countries themselves, as an act of aggression and therefore as clear evidence of a Soviet intention to subdue Western Europe unless prevented from doing so by countervailing force.

The second great change, related to and made possible by the first, is in the way the European countries to the east of Germany are governed. Virtually all have sought, with varying degrees of success, to install democratic political systems with governments popularly chosen in regular, free, fair elections that respect the rights of those they govern. Democracy reduces the chance of war because democracies are less susceptible than countries with other forms of government to the ambitions and drives that have for millennia produced international conflict. In Russia, while democracy is not firmly established, orthodox communism, which was highly susceptible to bellicose motives, has been damaged beyond repair.

The third change is in the military balance in Europe. A series of treaties has reshaped national military forces to make them more suitable for defense and less so for attack. The voluntary acceptance of treaty-imposed restraints on their own forces by each European country reassures all the others that none harbors aggressive designs. The restrictions themselves provide insurance in the event of the reappearance of such designs by making it difficult to carry them out. Any effort by a European country to escape the treaty-imposed limits on arms, moreover, would serve as a warning to others that the post-Cold War common security order was in jeopardy.

Common security reduces the insecurity that arises from the anarchy of the international system and historically has motivated the competitive amassing of military forces, making peace dependent on a balance of military power. The new order achieves peace without sharp political divisions among the major powers, at lower cost, lower risk, and lower levels of fear and uncertainty than ever before in Europe.

The North Atlantic Treaty Organization, one of the mainstays of the balance of power arrangement of the Cold War, also plays an integral part in this new security order. Post-Communist Europe is marked by transitions—from centrally planned to market economies and from Communist to democratic, or at least non-Communist, political systems. NATO, too, has undergone a transition in its principal mission, from deterrence to reassurance. The American commitment to Europe, for which NATO is the vehicle, reassures all the countries of the continent that sudden, sharp changes in the distribution of military might are not imminent. It reassures Germany's neighbors that the Germans will not feel the need to conduct an independent military policy, including the acquisition of nuclear weapons; at the same time, it reassures NATO's members, and others to the east, that if Russia should opt for the aggressive foreign policies of its imperial and Communist predecessors, the United States will remain the spine of a military coalition to oppose this, even as it was during the Cold War.

The common security order depends on the continuation of NATO's basic political arrangements; it would be jeopardized by either the contraction or the expansion of its membership, which would bring about dramatic changes in the role played in the new order by its two flanking powers, the United States and Russia.

As during the Cold War, the security of Europe depends in large measure on the policies of these two continental-sized, partly European countries, both of them heavily armed with nuclear weapons. During the Cold War, the commitment of each to offsetting the other's military power and political ambitions was unwavering—until the late 1980s and early 1990s when the Soviet side first voluntarily retreated and then involuntarily collapsed. In the wake of the Cold War, the participation of each in the new European common security order is in doubt.

What is in question in the American case is the country's commitment not to the norms of common security but rather to ongoing engagement in Europe's political and military affairs. The circumstance that drew the United States to Europe three times in the twentieth century, the threat of a single power dominating the continent, has vanished.

Still, in the second half of this century an American military presence of some kind in Europe has become normal; and there is no evidence of powerful public sentiment in the United States to withdraw completely.

The doubts in the Russian case involve not the country's role in Europe—which is, after all, a fact of geography—but the durability of its commitment to the tenets of common security. If subtracting the United States from the alliance would undercut the sense of confidence that the common security order promotes, expanding its formal membership eastward would risk destroying the legitimacy that the post-Cold War settlement has in Russian eyes.

Even without the expansion of NATO, Russia may withdraw from the new order. Nothing like the Western consensus in favor of the precepts of common security exists in the new Russia. But if there is reason for confidence that the United States will continue to be a European power, there is also reason for hope that Russia will continue to be a good citizen of Europe. Over the long term, it is possible that Russians will adhere to the norms of common security because they cannot conceive of breaking them; in the short term, it is likely that they will refrain from violating those norms because they are not strong enough to do so.

These post-Cold War security arrangements, which depend so heavily on the United States and Russia, do not represent the best of all imaginable ways of organizing the international relations of Europe. A Europe-wide government with an effective military force would offer a firmer guarantee against a major war and, unlike the common security order, could prevent lesser conflicts such as the wars in the former Yugoslavia. But the nation-states of Europe, old and new, will not surrender their sovereign prerogatives to a continental Leviathan. Europe would also be more secure if the common security order itself were more solidly established and deeply rooted. This, however, requires what by definition cannot be supplied quickly: the passage of time.

Therefore, in the crucial matter of the security of Europe—the heart of the international system and the scene of many of the bloodiest episodes in human history—a set of arrangements has emerged from the Cold War that embodies the best of all *possible* worlds. The policy wisdom that follows is a variation on Benjamin Franklin's reply to an onlooker who asked him, as he was leaving a meeting of the Constitutional Convention in Philadelphia, what the drafters had given the people of the world's newest independent country. "A republic," Franklin replied, "if you can keep it."[2]

Without benefit of a single grand meeting, but rather through dozens of separate negotiations each lasting thousands of hours, combined with unexpected, revolutionary political developments from Berlin to Vladivostok, by dint, that is, of hard work and good fortune, through both design and inadvertence, the governments of Europe and North America have provided the people of the European continent with a common security order. Their common task now is to keep it.

NOTES

1. Stephen F. Szabo, *The Diplomacy of German Unification* (New York: St. Martin's Press, 1992), p. 4, quoting Wolfram Hanrieder.

2. NATO began life as an anti-German creation. The Atlantic Alliance was an outgrowth of the Dunkirk Pact, which was signed by the British and French foreign ministers in 1947 with the explicit aim of resisting any sign of German revanchism. When the Benelux countries joined the pact in 1948, to make it the Brussels agreement, the explicit reference to Germany was dropped. It was the Brussels agreement to which the United States adhered in 1949, making it the North Atlantic Pact. Don Cook, *Forging the Alliance: NATO, 1945–50* (New York: Arbor House/William Morrow, 1989), pp. 75, 122, 259.

3. The document is quoted in Edward Mortimer, "In Search of a Unifying Threat," *Financial Times*, December 7, 1994, p. 15.

4. See chapter 5.

5. In 1995, French president Jacques Chirac offered to put France's nuclear arsenal, the mission of which French leaders had previously insisted was to protect France alone, at the service of the defense of all of Europe. He made the offer at least in part to deflect the criticism his country had attracted by its decision to conduct nuclear tests. The Germans expressed no enthusiasm for the idea.

6. As part of the terms of unification, the Germans agreed to limits on their military manpower and affirmed their renunciation, dating from the early days of the Federal Republic, of atomic, biological, and chemical weapons. Szabo, op. cit., p. 57.

7. See chapters 7 and 8.

8. Michael Howard, "Reassurance and Deterrence: Western Defense in the 1980s," *Foreign Affairs* 61, no. 2 (Winter 1982–83). See also Michael Mandelbaum, "The United States and the Strategic Quadrangle," in Mandelbaum, ed., *The Strategic Quadrangle: Russia, China, Japan and the United States in East Asia* (New York: The Council on Foreign Relations, 1995), p. 161.

9. On Russia, see chapter 7.

10. On the specific post-Cold War changes in NATO intended to create confidence, see pp. 101–2.

11. This subject is discussed in chapter 9.

12. "A credible American commitment to an alliance focused on territorial defense against a non-existent threat of massive conventional aggression from the East cannot long be politically sustained on Capitol Hill. If only for domestic political reasons, a new rationale for the alliance revolving around new missions and members appropriate to the new security environment in Europe may be essential to halting the erosion in support for NATO in Congress" Senator Richard G. Lugar, "NATO's 'Near Abroad': New Membership, New Missions" (Speech to the Atlantic Council of the United States, Washington, D.C., December 9, 1993), p. 18.

13. Senator Richard Lugar, "NATO: Out of Area or Out of Business: A Call for U.S. Leadership to Revive and Redefine the Alliance" (Remarks delivered at the Open Forum of the U.S. Department of State, August 2, 1993).

CHAPTER 2

1. Quoted in Ronald D. Asmus, "Germany's New Geopolitics" (Unpublished paper, Santa Monica, Calif.: The Rand Corporation, 1994), p. 26.

2. Even before the final collapse of the Soviet Union, in December 1991, NATO forces could be shifted to the Middle East without inviting an attack in Europe.

3. Stationing American forces permanently in Saudi Arabia to deter an Iraqi attack, as some in the Congress preferred, rather than actually launching them against the Iraqi garrison in Kuwait in order to evict it, as the Bush administration eventually did, would have served the larger strategic purpose of preventing Saddam Hussein from acquiring economic power that could have been converted into political leverage and military might on a dangerously large scale.

4. Preventing Saddam from acquiring nuclear weapons was an added incentive to go to war.

5. Susan L. Woodward, *Balkan Tragedy: Chaos and Dissolution after the Cold War* (Washington, D.C.: The Brookings Institution, 1995), p. 165.

6. Critics argued that air power alone would not have this effect, that ground troops were needed as well. The critics were proven right, although it was a Croatian not a Western army that, aided by a NATO air campaign against Serb military assets around Sarajevo and elsewhere, drove the Serbs out of some of the territory they had occupied when Yugoslavia had fallen apart.

7. The case that the Dayton accords create the illusion but not the reality of a united Bosnia is made in Robert Hayden, "Constitutionalism and Nationalism in the Balkans," *East European Constitutional Review* (Fall 1995).

8. See Woodward, op. cit., pp. 159, 184–85.

9. In 1878, the Western great powers intervened in the Balkans in part to forestall further Russian gains there. The same motive would have operated during the Cold War, but did not in its wake.

10. For "domino thinking" as characteristic of strong states in the international system, see Michael Mandelbaum, *The Fate of Nations: The Search for National Security in the Nineteenth and Twentieth Centuries* (New York: Cambridge University Press, 1988), chapter 3.

11. Even during the Cold War, when the image of falling dominoes was potent, it was not NATO but the United States that tried to stop dangerous chain reactions through interventions outside Europe, often, as in Vietnam, without the support of its European allies. Even during the Cold War, when solidarity was at a premium and the world a dangerous place, NATO did not undertake out-of-area missions. See Elizabeth D. Sherwood, *Allies in Crisis: Meeting Global Challenges to Western Security* (New Haven: Yale University Press, 1990).

12. See Richard H. Ullman, *Securing Europe* (Princeton, N.J.: Princeton University Press, 1989), pp. 27–29, 144.

13. In the two major American wars during the Cold War, in Korea and Vietnam, public support dropped as casualties rose. See John Mueller, *War, Presidents, and Public Opinion* (New York: John Wiley, 1973).

14. Thus former president Jimmy Carter, retired general Colin Powell, and Senator Sam Nunn of Georgia were dispatched to the island to persuade the ruling junta to leave peacefully, ensuring that American troops would not meet armed opposition.

15. Deputy Secretary of State Strobe Talbott, quoted in Adam Garfinkle, "Into the Shooting Gallery," *The National Interest* 42 (Winter 1995–96), p. 119.

16. Woodward, op. cit., p. 273.

17. See chapter 8.

18. See chapter 1.

CHAPTER 3

1. The term comes from the town of Visegrad, located in Hungary north of Budapest, where the presidents of Poland, Hungary, and Czechoslovakia (as it then was) met on February 15, 1991, to discuss economic cooperation among their countries.

2. Quoted in Michael Dobbs, "Wider Alliance Would Increase U.S. Commitments," *The Washington Post*, July 5, 1995, p. A16. House Resolution 7, passed by the 104th Congress, stipulated that the Visegrad Four should enter NATO no later than January 10, 1999.

3. Dobbs, op. cit., p. A16.

4. Michael Dobbs, "Domestic Political Costs Will Mount after the Rhetoric Is Spent," *The Washington Post*, July 7, 1995, p. A1.

5. The Clinton administration said that NATO will not have different classes of members, some with and some without an American nuclear commitment. In fact, the Visegrad Four already received a measure of protection from NATO even while remaining outside the organization's formal framework, just as the European neutrals did during the Cold War. See Michael Mandelbaum, *The Fate of Nations: The Search for National Security in the Nineteenth and Twentieth Centuries* (New York: Cambridge University Press, 1988), pp. 202–3.

6. See chapter 1.

7. ". . . the British are very wary of NATO's assuming a global policeman role and of accepting new members, but recognize that it is necessary to take steps in those directions. One could almost characterize official views of new members as 'a bad idea whose time has come.'" Robert P. Grant, *The Changing Franco-American Security Relationship: New Directions for NATO and European Defense Cooperation*, A Symposium Report (Arlington, Va.: U.S.-CREST [Center for Research and Education on Strategy and Technology], December 1993), p. 39.

". . . early enlargement [of NATO] would be offered only to those central European states that need it least; and any attempt to revive the Russian threat as Nato's *raison d'etre* so long as the threat is not unmistakable, is more likely to divide the alliance than to unite it. West European governments can already be heard expressing caution. . . ." Edward Mortimer, "In search of a unifying threat," *Financial Times*, December 7, 1994, p. 15.

8. On the prospects and implications for foreign policy of democracy in Russia, see chapter 7.

9. Bruce Clark and George Graham, "Work Begins on a New Wing," *Financial Times*, December 1, 1994, p. 12. See also Dobbs, "Wider Alliance," p. A16.

10. Asmus, op. cit., pp. 28–29.

11. Secretary Christopher, "Transforming the NATO Alliance to Meet New Security Needs," Intervention before the ministerial meeting of the North Atlantic Council, Istanbul, Turkey, June 9, 1994, U.S. State Department Dispatch, Vol. 5, No. 24, p. 1.

12. The one country of the four with a sizable ethnic minority was Slovakia, where 400,000 Hungarians lived. A treaty guaranteeing their rights was signed by the two countries in 1995. This was cited by Clinton administration officials as evidence of the constructive power of the *prospect* of NATO membership, which they credited with encouraging the accord. See Strobe Talbott, "Why NATO Should Grow," *The New York Review of Books*, August 10, 1995, p. 4. The rights in question included the use of the Hungarian language in Slovakia. While it is surely desirable for the Hungarian citizens of Slovakia to have access to newspapers, school instruction, and street signs in their native language, this is an odd goal for Western security policy.

13. See Rick Atkinson and John Pomfret, "East Looks to NATO to Forge Links to West," *The Washington Post*, July 6, 1995, p. A24,

and Jim Hoagland, "NATO: The Case for Holding Back," *The Washington Post*, June 22, 1995, p. A31. For a different interpretation, see Stephen Sestanovich, "The Collapsing Partnership," in Robert J. Lieber, ed., *Eagle Adrift: American Foreign Policy at the End of the Century* (New York: Longman, forthcoming).

14. Peter Rodman, "4 More for NATO," *The Washington Post*, December 13, 1994, p. A27.

15. Ibid. "Russia is authoritarian at heart and expansionist by habit; with its educated population and vast resources—now unencumbered by Communist baggage—Russia will rise again to superpowerhood, and it is manifestly destined to look west and south to fill its irredental caries." William Safire, "A Strategic Dilemma," *The New York Times*, December 1, 1994, p. A33.

16. Americans with roots in newly independent former Soviet republics reportedly lobbied in favor of NATO expansion "on the understanding that their nations will be next in line." Atkinson and Pomfret, op. cit. There was, however, no evidence that NATO's member governments seriously contemplated admitting them.

17. The Lithuanian government took the position that it would need special arrangements with NATO in the event of an eastward expansion of the alliance that did not include them. Jeffrey Simon, "NATO Enlargement," *Strategic Focus* no. 31, (Washington, The National Defense University, May 1995), p. 3. The Ukrainian government's position was equivocal. Kiev was wary of offending either the West or Russia.

18. See Timothy Garton Ash, *The Polish Revolution: Solidarity* (New York: Charles Scribner's Sons, 1983), p. 1.

19. See chapter 7.

20. Henry Kissinger, "Not This Partnership," *The Washington Post*, November 24, 1993, p. A17.

21. "Russia and NATO," Theses of the Council on Foreign and Defense Policy, the membership of which is described as consisting of "well-known experts, members of the Parliament, high-ranking officials from the foreign policy and 'power' (defense, interior and security) agencies [acting] in their personal capacity." Moscow, May 25, 1995, p. 1 (English translation).

22. Ibid., p. 4. The conclusion was not confined to Russian analysts. "No matter how artfully NATO manages to disguise it, NATO expansion will signify to most Russians, including those

most committed to Western values and institutions, the drawing of a new line in Europe that establishes which states the West is geared up to include and which not. It will further discredit in Russian eyes the West's talk about integrating Russia fully into the community of industrial democracies and lend weight to the argument that Russia cannot afford to pursue a modernization strategy that depends critically on its integration into the West. . . . Larger sections of the Russian elite will conclude that Russia, if it is not to settle for isolation on the fringe of Europe, must therefore find a different, uniquely Russian place for itself in the world. . . ." Arnold L. Horelick, "U.S. Interests in Europe and NATO Enlargement," Prepared statement for a hearing before the European Subcommittee of the Foreign Relations Committee of the United States Senate, April 27, 1995; reprinted by the Rand Corporation, Rand Testimony Series Number CT–131.

23. See chapter 8.

24. Quoted in Rodman, ibid., and Michael Lind, "Let's Appease Russia," *The New Republic*, January 9 and 16, 1995, p. 28.

25. Quoted in John Thornhill, "Yeltsin Warns Nato of 'flames of war,'" *Financial Times*, Weekend September 9/10, 1995, p. 2.

26. One Western response to Russian objections was to assert that the circle would be squared: expansion would take place in a way that would not subvert good relations with Russia, which would be offered a "special relationship" of unspecified character with the alliance. See Zbigniew Brzezinski, "A Plan for Europe," *Foreign Affairs*, January-February 1995, p. 34, and Henry Kissinger, "Expand NATO Now," *The Washington Post*, December 19, 1994, p. A27.

27. According to Sergei Karaganov, an adviser to President Boris Yeltsin, if "NATO expands eastward, Russia under any government will become a revisionist power striving to undermine the already fragile European order." Quoted in Charles A. Kupchan, "Expand NATO—And Split Europe," *The New York Times*, November 27, 1994, p. 11.

28. The Allies' post-World War I policy toward Germany involved a fatal combination: harsh treatment without occupation. This turned Germany against the settlement without ensuring that it would be unable to act on its opposition. The post-World War II settlement featured the opposite combination: generous treatment of the Germans, at least by the Western powers,

in concert with prolonged military occupation. NATO expansion risks repeating the first disastrous combination. There is an important difference. After World War I, the leaders of the victorious powers had little room to maneuver in dealing with Germany. At the postwar Paris Peace Conference, they were under pressure from their own publics to impose harsh terms that would justify the enormous sacrifices in blood and treasure that had been necessary to win the war. Western leaders in the post-Cold War period are under no such pressure. See Mandelbaum, op. cit., pp. 62–63.

29. Later scholarship has generally concluded that imperial Germany did bear the major responsibility for the outbreak of war in 1914. The best-known post-1919 argument that the reparations imposed on Germany were economically ruinous to pay, which was made by John Maynard Keynes in his book *The Economic Consequences of the Peace* (New York: Brace and Howe, 1920), was disputed by the Frenchman Etienne Mantoux in *The Carthaginian Peace: Or the Economic Consequencs of Mr. Keynes* (New York: Oxford University Press, 1946).

30. Bill Clinton and Boris Yeltsin, "Joint Statement on European Security," Moscow, May 10, 1995, p. 1.

31. Stephen F. Szabo, *The Diplomacy of German Unification* (New York: St. Martin's Press, 1992), p. 65. See also the earlier proposal of German foreign minister Hans-Dietrich Genscher, ibid., pp. 57–58, and NATO's subsequent "London Declaration," ibid., p. 92.

32. See Dobbs, "Wider Alliance," p. A16. See also the quote from President Vaclav Havel of the Czech Republic in Jonathan Dean, *Ending Europe's Wars: The Continuing Search for Peace and Security* (New York: Twentieth Century Fund Press, 1993), p. 122.

CHAPTER 4

1. Cited in Kenneth N. Waltz, *Man, the State, and War* (New York, Columbia University Press, 1954), pp. 210–11. As Waltz put it, "Because any state may at any time use force, all states must constantly be ready either to counter force with force or to pay the cost of weakness. The requirements of state action are, in this view, imposed by the circumstances in which all states exist." Ibid., p. 160.

2. "There is in international politics no simple rule to prescribe just how belligerent, or how peaceful, any given state should

strive to appear in order to maximize its chances of living at peace with neighboring states." Waltz, op. cit., p. 222. See also Michael Mandelbaum, *The Fate of Nations*, (New York: Cambridge University Press, 1988), chapter 6.

3. Rousseau believed that such wars were common: "everyone, having no guarantee that he can avoid war, is anxious to begin it at the moment which suits his own interest and so forestall a neighbor, who would not fail to forestall the attack in his turn at any moment favorable to himself, so that many wars, even offensive wars, are rather in the nature of unjust precautions for the protection of the assailant's own possessions than a device for seizing those of others." Quoted in Waltz, op. cit., p. 180. The term political scientists use for the poisonous interaction of misperceptions is "the spiral model." See Robert Jervis, *Perception and Misperception in International Politics* (Princeton, N.J.: Princeton University Press, 1976), chapter 3; and Mandelbaum, op. cit., pp. 254–62.

4. Thucydides, *The Peloponnesian War*, trans. Rex Warner (Harmondsworth, England: Penguin Books, 1972), p. 49.

5. On the origins of the post-1945 Soviet-American conflict see, for example, Arthur Schlesinger, Jr., "Origins of the Cold War," *Foreign Affairs* 46, no. 1 (October 1967). On the Sino-American conflict, see Allen S. Whiting, *China Crosses the Yalu* (New York: Macmillian, 1960).

6. For the argument that a balance is easier to strike with two than with more than two powers see Kenneth N. Waltz, *Theory of International Politics* (Reading, Mass.: Addison-Wesley, 1979), chapter 8. On the balance of power in the nuclear age see Michael Mandelbaum, *The Nuclear Revolution* (New York: Cambridge University Press, 1981), chapter 3.

7. This is a theme of Paul Kennedy, *The Rise and Fall of the Great Powers* (New York: Random House, 1987).

8. As defined here, common security shares a number of features with what has been called "cooperative security." See Janne E. Nolan, ed., *Global Engagement: Cooperation and Security in the 21st Century* (Washington, D.C.: The Brookings Institution, 1994).

9. On the withering of "state-level" motives for war in the second half of the twentieth century, see Richard H. Ullman, *Securing Europe* (Princeton, N.J.: Princeton University Press, 1991), and John Mueller, *Retreat from Doomsday: The Obsolescence of Major War* (New York: Basic Books, 1989).

10. The belief did not die out with the nineteenth century. According to British prime minister John Major, "trade is a peacemaker, one of the most powerful and persuasive." Quoted in K.J. Holsti, "The Post-War 'Settlement' in Comparative Perspective," in Douglas T. Stuart and Stephen F. Szabo, eds., *Discord and Collaboration in a New Europe* (Washington, D.C.: The Foreign Policy Institute, The Paul H. Nitze School of Advanced International Studies of The Johns Hopkins University, 1994), p. 56.

11. Kant believed that the combination of representative government and the painful lessons of recurrent warfare would eventually lead to perpetual peace.

12. This has become something like an article of post-Cold War faith in the West. Thus President Bill Clinton: "Ultimately, the best strategy to ensure our security and to build a durable peace is to support the advance of democracy elsewhere. Democracies don't attack each other." Similarly, British prime minister Margaret Thatcher: "If we can create a great area of democracy stretching from the west coast of the United States . . . to the Far East, that would give us the best guarantee of all for security— because democracies don't go to war with one another." (Both quoted in "Democracies and War: the Politics of Peace," *The Economist*, April 1, 1995, p. 17).

13. Rousseau held a similar view. Monarchies, he thought, were bellicose because monarchs profited from war, while their subjects, who did not, had no say in the decision to fight.

14. The issue is discussed in the essays in Michael E. Brown, Sean M. Lynn-Jones, and Steven E. Miller, eds., *Debating the Democratic Peace* (Cambridge, Mass.: The MIT Press, 1996).

15. Wilson had a formula for promoting democracy: national self-determination. Here the record is mixed. Not all sovereign states are ethnically homogeneous; not all states that are homogeneous are democratic; and not all democracies consist overwhelmingly of a single ethnic or national group.

CHAPTER 5

1. The others include Mikhail Gorbachev's announcement, in December 1988, of a unilateral Soviet decision to reduce its deployed forces by 500,000, the Conventional Forces in Europe

(CFE) Treaty in November 1990, the first Strategic Arms Reduction Treaty (START I) of July 1991, reciprocal unilateral decisions to reduce sharply Soviet and American deployments of tactical nuclear weapons by Presidents Bush and Gorbachev in October and November 1991, respectively, and a Bush-Yeltsin accord on "Open Skies" in March 1992.

2. This was not true of the numerical limits on nuclear weapons. Most European governments did not have such weapons and Great Britain and France, which did have them, were not parties to the INF accords.

3. On the symbolic importance of the earlier arms control accords, see Michael Mandelbaum, "The Reagan Administration and the Nature of Arms Control," in Joseph Kruzel, ed., *American Defense Annual, 1988–89* (Lexington, Mass.: Lexington Books, 1988), p. 201. The rationale for Cold War arms control talks was memorably expressed by Churchill: "Better jaw-jaw than war-war." The phrase implies what the history of international relations does not always bear out: if parties are arguing and negotiating they will not be fighting. Pre-1987 arms control may be compared to the bumper sticker that reads, "I brake for animals." The slogan is a sign of the state of mind of the driver, not a safety feature of the car. Of course, the safety with which a car is driven depends, first and foremost, on the state of mind of the driver, and this is also the case for international conflicts. Where the familiar state-level causes of war are concerned, wars do, as the saying goes, begin in the minds of men.

4. On the contribution of the events of 1989 and 1991 to the disappearance of state-level causes, see chapter 7.

5. American officials arbitrarily designated the level that would be unacceptable as 50 percent of the Soviet Union's industrial capacity and 25 percent of its population. Michael Mandelbaum, *The Nuclear Question: The United States and Nuclear Weapons, 1946–1976* (New York: Cambridge University Press, 1979), p. 85.

6. In advocating strategic defense, Reagan was rhetorically faithful to the spirit of common security. He asserted that, once the technology of defense had been developed, the United States would share it with the Soviet Union. The Soviet leadership showed no sign of believing him.

7. The pre-treaty totals were 1,968 for the United States and 2,568 for the Soviet Union.

8. When the United States Senate ratified START II on January 26, 1996, the Russian Duma had yet to do so. The Lisbon Protocol of May 23, 1992, consolidated and confined to Russia the nuclear weapons of the former Soviet Union, thereby reinforcing mutual assured destruction by limiting the number of nuclear weapon states.

9. Specifically, the treaty provided for the elimination of 1,600 ballistic and cruise missiles, with ranges of between 1,000 and 5,000 kilometers, including 900 deployed in NATO Europe and the Soviet Union, which had been the subject of negotiations since the late 1970s. It also provided for the elimination of approximately 1,000 additional shorter-range (500–1,000 kilometers) missile systems, which had not been included in the earlier talks. It thus became known as the "double-zero" treaty.

10. As a result, only some air-delivered nuclear weapons of tactical range remained outside the borders of the United States. Leonard S. Spector and Jonathan Dean, "Cooperative Security: Assessing the Tools of the Trade," in Janne E. Nolan, ed., *Global Engagement: Cooperation and Security in the 21st Century* (Washington, D.C.: The Brookings Institution, 1994), p. 139. Tactical nuclear weapons continued to be deployed in Russia east of the Ural Mountains.

11. The fact of the Warsaw Pact's nonnuclear superiority was widely but not universally accepted in the West. For a dissenting view, see John Mearsheimer, *Conventional Deterrence* (Ithaca, N.Y.: Cornell University Press, 1983), chapter 6.

12. The term "conventional" weapons was coined to distinguish them from nuclear armaments. As the term implied, they were and are a familiar and traditional part of the history of warfare, for which there are conventions of usage and tactical rules that are lacking for the newer and more powerful nuclear weapons.

13. The United States entered the MBFR talks as a way to oppose an effort in Congress to reduce the number of American troops stationed in Europe through the "Mansfield Amendment," introduced by the Democratic Senate majority leader Mike Mansfield in 1972. The Soviet government was not subject to similar pressure, but could not appear to be indifferent to the cause of arms reduction. Each side thus had an interest in not blocking negotiations but also in not bringing them to a conclusion in a treaty. As with the treaties concluded before 1987, the purpose of these negotiations was to a large extent cosmetic.

14. Conventional weapons were less usable in Europe than elsewhere during the Cold War because their use had a greater potential in Europe than elsewhere for triggering the use of nuclear weapons.

15. Specifically, CFE permitted NATO and the Warsaw Pact 20,000 tanks, 30,000 armored vehicles, 20,000 artillery pieces, 6,800 combat aircraft, and 2,000 attack helicopters. Cited in Spurgeon Keeney, Jr., "Arms Control During the Transition to the post-Cold War World," in Joseph Kruzel, ed., *American Defense Annual, 1993* (Lexington, Mass.: Lexington Books, 1993), p. 193.

16. Jonathan Dean, *Ending Europe's Wars: The Continuing Search for Peace and Security* (New York: Twentieth Century Fund Press, 1994), p. 291.

17. Ibid., p. 299.

18. Ibid.

19. Ibid., p. 306. "It is possible to imagine . . . common standards for the density of forces . . . concentration . . . movement . . . and transparency. If international rules were established in these terms, the major ground force establishments could be set in configurations that are reasonably accepted as defensive." Ashton B. Carter, William J. Perry, and John D. Steinbruner, *A New Concept of Cooperative Security* (Washington, D.C.: The Brookings Institution, 1992), p. 23.

20. An understanding known as "CFE 1A," imposing limits on military personnel, was signed in July 1992. It did not have the status of a formal treaty because the Western signatories believed that it could not be verified with absolute confidence. In addition, in June 1991, the Soviet government made a series of commitments, which the successor Russian regime inherited, about the weapons that had been moved east of the Urals to evade CFE limits: to destroy some, not to use the rest to create new operational units, and to provide information about the remaining armaments on a continuing basis. Dean, op. cit., pp. 299–301.

21. Ibid., p. 294. See also pp. 260–310.

22. Ibid., p. 294. "But total Russian tanks, including those deployed and stored east of the Urals, are much more numerous. The International Institute for Strategic Studies estimates the total as close to 50,000."

23. On the significance of Russian-Ukrainian relations, see chapter 8.

CHAPTER 6

1. On the Paris accords, see Lewis Dunn, "Arms Control: Looking Back, Looking Ahead," in Joseph Kruzel, ed., *American Defense Annual, 1991–92* (Lexington, Mass.: Lexington Books, 1992), p. 168; on Vienna, see Jonathan Dean, *Ending Europe's Wars: The Continuing Search for Peace and Security* (New York: Twentieth Century Fund Press, 1994), pp. 319–21.

2. Richard K. Betts, *Surprise Attack* (Washington, D.C.: The Brookings Institution, 1982), p. 18.

3. When the Soviet Union disintegrated, its former republics, which became independent states, became eligible to take part as well.

4. See above, pp. 82–84.

5. See Timothy Garton Ash, *In Europe's Name: Germany and the Divided Continent* (New York: Random House, 1993), pp. 315–20.

6. Walter Slocombe, a Defense Department official in the Carter and later the Clinton administrations, quoted in Strobe Talbott, *Deadly Gambits: The Reagan Administration and the Stalemate in Nuclear Arms Control* (New York: Knopf, 1984), p. 333.

7. On Gorbachev and common security, see chapter 7.

8. On the Concert of Europe as a collective approach to security, see Michael Mandelbaum, *The Fate of Nations: The Search for National Security in the Nineteenth and Twentieth Centuries* (New York: Cambridge University Press, 1988), chapter 1. Strictly speaking, the Concert began as the Quadruple Alliance of 1815, which was followed by what was known as the "Congress system," in which a number of important European meetings were convened and which gave way to the less formal, less frequent arrangements that became known as the Concert of Europe.

9. In the post-Cold War era the candidate for that role is the United States. See chapter 9.

CHAPTER 7

1. The distinction in this context comes from Fritz Ermarth.

2. This is a major theme of Coit D. Blacker, *Hostage to Revolution: Gorbachev and Soviet Security Policy, 1985–1991* (New York: The Council on Foreign Relations, 1993). See also Eugene Rumer, *Russian National Security and Foreign Policy in Transition* (Santa Monica, Calif.: Rand, 1995), p. 5.

3. Quoted in Raymond L. Garthoff, *Deterrence and the Revolution in Soviet Military Doctrine* (Washington, D.C.: The Brookings Institution, 1990), p. 135.

4. Mikhail Gorbachev, *Perestroika: New Thinking for Our Country and the World* (New York: Harper and Row, 1987), p. 142.

5. Ibid.

6. Ibid., p. 141.

7. Garthoff, op. cit., pp. 119–20.

8. Ibid.

9. Gorbachev, op. cit., pp. 142–43.

10. Ibid., p. 203.

11. Ibid.

12. Ibid., p. 204.

13. Rumer, op. cit., pp. 8, 10.

14. Ibid., pp. vii, 23.

15. Ibid., p. 24, quoting Yevgeny Ambartsumov, one-time chairman of the Foreign Affairs Committee of the Russian Federation Supreme Soviet.

16. See below, pp. 150–52.

17. The view was shared by those who lived involuntarily under Communist rule, as the periodic uprisings demonstrated.

18. The need to control Central and Eastern Europe politically was also arguably the basis for the Warsaw Pact's threatening military posture. See above, p. 91.

19. It was Gorbachev who repealed the so-called Brezhnev Doctrine, according to which Eastern Europe would have to remain forever Communist. The change was all but announced in 1987: "Universal security in our time rests on the recognition of the right of every nation to choose its own path of social development, on the renunciation of interference in the domestic affairs of other states . . . A nation may choose either capitalism or socialism. This is its sovereign right." Gorbachev, op. cit., p. 143. In 1989 the Eastern Europeans took these words seriously enough to act on them, and Gorbachev allowed them to do so.

20. "X" (George F. Kennan), "The Source of Soviet Conduct," *Foreign Affairs* 23 (July 1947), p. 572.

21. Roderic Braithwaite, "Russia's Future and Western Policy," in Robert Blackwill, Roderick Braithwaite, and Akihiko Tanaka, *Engaging Russia* (New York: The Trilateral Commission, 1995), p. 78.

22. For an argument that "reform communism" was an oxymoron, that there was no middle ground between Brezhnevite

orthodoxy and collapse, see Martin Malia, *The Soviet Tragedy: A History of Socialism in Russia, 1917–1991* (New York: The Free Press, 1994).

23. Kenneth N. Waltz, *Man, the State, and War* (New York: Columbia University Press, 1959), pp. 180–81.

24. Not all market economies are democracies; all democracies in the modern era, however, have had market economies.

25. This view may be taking root in post-Soviet Russia, where neoimperialist rhetoric must contend with concern about the costs of acting on it. (See Rumer, op. cit., p. viii.) In particular, there was opposition to the absorption of Belarus based on the anticipated drain on Russian finances. The desire to control territory and the willingness to use force to do so are not extinct in Europe, as the grim events of the 1990s in the former Yugoslavia illustrate. Whatever else may be said about it, however, the Balkan ethnic cleansing—the forced expulsion of people of particular religious and national backgrounds—was not undertaken with an eye toward economic gain.

26. The presumed connection between interdependence and nonbelligerence was the premise underlying the economic cooperation in Western Europe that began shortly after World War II and culminated in the establishment and development of the European Union. France and Germany had fought three wars in seventy years. If the citizens of each came to depend significantly on the other for their well-being, the founders of European cooperation believed, there would not be a fourth war. There has been none, and Franco-German cooperation became the keystone of the politics and economics of post-1945 Western Europe.

27. These economies had been highly interdependent in the Communist era, but this was a different, unnatural, uneconomic interdependence, based on the arbitrary decisions of government planners.

28. For contrasting views of the impact of such traditions, see Stephen Holmes, "Cultural Legacies or State Collapse? Probing the Postcommunist Dilemma" and Charles Gati, "If Not Democracy, What? Leaders, Laggards, and Losers in the Postcommunist World," in Michael Mandelbaum, ed., *Postcommunism: Four Perspectives* (New York: The Council on Foreign Relations, 1996).

29. Leon Aron, "The Emergent Priorities of Russian Foreign Policy," in Leon Aron and Kenneth M. Jensen, eds., *The Emergence*

of Russian Foreign Policy (Washington, D.C.: The United States Institute of Peace Press, 1994), p. 18.

30. This is the argument of Edward D. Mansfield and Jack Snyder, "Democratization and War," *Foreign Affairs*, May/June 1995, in particular p. 88.

CHAPTER 8

1. Eugene Rumer, *Russian National Security and Foreign Policy in Transition* (Santa Monica, Calif.: Rand, 1995), p. 37.

2. Ibid., p. 22.

3. This was the definition of the Russian nation and the vision of the Russian future articulated by Alexander Solzhenitsyn, who emphasized, however, that the reassociation of the Slavic peoples had to be accomplished nonviolently.

4. The separation of Ukraine from Russia has thus far been much less violent than the war of independence in North America in the last quarter of the eighteenth century and the partition of the Asian subcontinent in 1947.

5. Rumer, op. cit., p. 28. According to Boris Yeltsin, "future integration cannot cost Russia. . . ." Quoted in Martha Brill Olcott, "Sovereignty and the 'Near Abroad,'" *Orbis* 39, no. 3 (Summer 1995), p. 364.

6. See above, p. 122–23.

7. Stephen M. Meyer, "Russian Security Relations with the Newly Independent States" (National Intelligence Council Conference on Prospects for the Space of the Former Soviet Union, Washington, D.C., March 23, 1995, draft discussion paper), p. 2.

8. It was also an army that, for this particular mission, lacked public support. The war was unpopular, perhaps a hopeful sign for the future of Russian participation in the common security order.

9. This is one reason that the expansion of NATO was not, in 1996, a matter of urgency. See chapter 3.

10. In the late 1980s, China dropped almost all of its territorial claims against the Soviet Union. Andrew A. Bouchkin, "Russia's Far Eastern Policy in the 1990: Problems and Prospects," in Adeed Dawisha and Karen Dawisha, eds., *The Making of Foreign Policy in Russia and the New States of Eurasia* (Armonk, New York: M.E. Sharpe, 1995), p. 73.

11. The border skirmishes of that year remain the only shooting war thus far between two countries both armed with nuclear weapons.

12. "In 1993 alone transboundary trade amounted to $2.5 billion, with a total of 2.5 million people crossing the border." Bouchkin, op. cit., p. 73.

13. See Robert Legvold, "Russia and the Strategic Quadrangle," in Michael Mandelbaum, ed., *The Strategic Quadrangle: Russia, China, Japan and the United States in East Asia* (New York: The Council on Foreign Relations, 1995), pp. 50–51; and David M. Lampton, "China and the Strategic Quadrangle," in ibid., p. 84.

14. Similarly, when Russia's relations with the West came under strain, Russian officials began discussing improving relations with China and Boris Yeltsin made a state visit to Beijing in April 1996.

15. Ivan Korotchenya, Russian executive director of the Commonwealth of Independent States, speaking on May 22, 1995, quoted in Robert Blackwill, "The Context of Russian Foreign Policy," in Robert Blackwill, Roderick Braithwaite, and Akihiko Tanaka, *Engaging Russia* (New York: The Trilateral Commission, 1995), p. 9.

16. Leon Aron, "The Emergent Priorities of Russian Foreign Policy," in Leon Aron and Kenneth M. Jensen, eds., *The Emergence of Russian Foreign Policy* (Washington, D.C.: The United States Institute of Peace, 1994), p. 29. While President James Monroe declared in 1823 that other powers were not welcome in the Western Hemisphere, the Russian version asserted a special role for Russia; such a role for the United States was perhaps implied by the original Monroe Doctrine but was not proclaimed as such.

17. Olcott, op. cit., pp. 357, 359.

18. Kemal H. Karpat, "The Central Asian States' Foreign Policy," in Dawisha and Dawisha, eds., op. cit., p. 203.

19. Blackwill, op. cit., p. 9.

20. One Russian official compared Russia's relations with its southern neighbors to French policy in sub-Saharan Africa. Jonathan Valdez, "Russia, the Near Abroad, and the West," in Dawisha and Dawisha, eds., op. cit., p. 104.

21. Such efforts would likely meet with resistance. See Karen Dawisha, "Imperialism, Dependence, and Interdependence in

the Eurasian Space," in ibid., p. 343. The three terms together accurately characterize the mixed Russian policy to its south.

22. Quoted in Aron, op. cit., p. 28. See also Blackwill, op. cit., p. 13.

23. Mark N. Katz, "Emerging Patterns in the International Relations of Central Asia," in Dawsisha and Dawisha, eds., op. cit., p. 249.

24. This is how, by the end of the nineteenth century, Britain acquired an empire so vast that the sun never set on it. The locus classicus for an account of this particular dynamic, the "imperialism of the turbulent frontier," is Ronald Robinson and John Gallagher, *Africa and the Victorians* (New York: St. Martin's Press, 1961). On "domino thinking" of this kind see chapter 2.

25. In June 1996, an agreement was reached modifying the CFE southern flank limit to facilitate Russian compliance.

CHAPTER 9

1. Quoted in Harold Temperley, *The Foreign Policy of Canning, 1822–27* (London: G. Bell and Sons, 1925), p. 154.

2. This was Gorbachev's view. See Stephen F. Szabo, *The Diplomacy of German Unification* (New York: St. Martin's Press, 1992), p. 99. According to a private Russian group, the Council on Foreign and Defense Policy, "Russia is . . . interested in the existence of NATO in its current capacity as a guarantor of stability in the relations along the West-West axis, and also in reforming and strengthening it as a reliable mechanism of European stability that can become one of the pillars of the new collective security architecture of the continent. The North Atlantic Treaty Organization as a defensive military and political union of democratic states is not a military threat for a democratic Russia." "Russia and NATO" (Theses of the Council on Foreign And Defense Policy, Moscow, May 25, 1995), p. 4; translated from the Russian.

3. "While the current defense budget of $253 billion is down fractionally from the previous year, it is still 85 percent of the average Cold War level. This makes it as large as that of all the other nations of the world *combined*. . . . The cost of 'reassuring' allies does not come cheap. Currently it costs $100 billion a year for

Europe, and another $46 billion for Japan and South Korea. Today more than 50 percent of all discretionary federal spending is still devoted to defense, even in the absence of an enemy." Ronald Steel, *Temptations of a Superpower* (Cambridge, Mass.: Harvard University Press, 1995), pp. 52, 60.

4. Cited in Ted Galen Carpenter, *Beyond NATO: Staying Out of Europe's Wars* (Washington, D.C.: The Cato Institute, 1994), p. 144. Carpenter is skeptical that NATO in its Cold War form is needed in the post-Cold War era.

5. On this point, see David P. Calleo, *Beyond American Hegemony: The Future of the Western Alliance* (New York: Basic Books, 1987), pp. 34–35. This was George Kennan's fear at the outset of the Cold War. See John Harper, *American Visions of Europe* (New York: Cambridge University Press, 1994), chapter 5.

6. Steel, op. cit., p. 35.

7. The principal source is John E. Rielly, ed., *American Public Opinion and U.S. Foreign Policy 1995* (Chicago: The Chicago Council on Foreign Relations, 1995).

8. Ibid., pp. 6, 10, 38.

9. Ibid., p. 28.

10. Ibid., pp. 6, 13.

11. Ibid., p. 7.

12. Ibid., pp. 12, 14.

13. Ibid., pp. 35–36.

14. A change of government in Washington accelerated each increase in defense spending, from the Eisenhower to the Kennedy administration in 1961 and from the Carter to the Reagan administration in 1981.

15. Carpenter, op. cit., p. 21. Don Cook, *Forging the Alliance* (New York: Arbor House/ William Morrow, 1989), p. 226.

CONCLUSION

1. Quoted in Ronald Steel, *Temptations of a Superpower* (Cambridge, Mass.: Harvard University Press, 1995), p. 83.

2. Quoted in Richard Brookhiser, *Founding Father: Rediscovering George Washington* (New York: The Free Press, 1996), p. 122.

INDEX

About the Author

Michael Mandelbaum is the Christian A. Herter Professor of American Foreign Policy at The Paul H. Nitze School of Advanced International Studies of The Johns Hopkins University and director of the Project on East-West Relations at the Council on Foreign Relations.